Philosophical Streets

Urbs et Orbi: The Urban Project, Volume 1

Air-Shaft Tunnel, Val Lewton. 2nd & Massachusetts Ave., NW, Washington D.C.

We have learned to practice *trompe l'oeil* (literally, "to delude the eye") as a political act—an act of faith in the incessant stream of photo opportunities and third-order simulations which are now the first reality of the postmodern city as "semio-scape" (*see* Arthur Kroker, "Sign Crimes," *The Postmodern Scene*. Montréal: New World Perspectives, 1986).

Philosophical Streets

New Approaches

To Urbanism

Edited by

Dennis Crow

Urbs et Orbi: The Urban Project, Volume 1

MAISONNEUVE PRESS

Institute for Advanced Cultural Studies

Acknowledgments. The editor wishes to thank the following publishers and copyright holders for permission to reprint certain materials:

Telos Press for "Culture and Administration"
Sage Publications for "Le Corbusier's Post-Modern Plan"
MIT Press for "In The Museyroom"
Los Angeles County Museum of Art for "Ceci n'est pas une pipe"
Agus Rusli for "Success. . . ."
Harvard GSD for James Tilghman's "Discontinuity. . . ."
M. Christine Boyer for "The Return of Aesthetics to City Planning"

●

Maisonneuve Press
is a division of the Institute for Advanced Cultural Studies, a non-profit collective of scholars concerned with the critical study of culture. Write to the Director for information about Institute programs.

Printed in the U.S. by BookCrafters, Fredricksburg, VA.
Manufactured to exceed the standards of the Committee on Production Guidelines for Book Longevity of the Council on Library Resources.

Cover photo by Dennis Crow: Austin, TX.

Library of Congress Cataloging-in-Publication Data
main entry under title
Philosophical streets: new approaches to urbanism
edited by Dennis Crow.
p. 173 -- (Urbs et orbi ; v. 1)
Includes bibliographical references; index.
1. City planning -- History -- 20th century. 2. Architecture, Postmodern. I. Series.
NA9095.P48 1990   90-5623
307.1'216'0904--dc20   CIP
ISBN 0-944624-08-1 (cloth)
ISBN 0-944624-09-X (paper)

To the light and love of my parents
Grant B. and Jen R. Crow

I would like to thank the authors for their interest, effort and patience. Many other people have been involved in reading early drafts of the essays: Charles Hoch, Christine Boyer, Larry Hickman, and Lawrence Grossberg. Inspiration for the topical and political purpose of this book has come from conversations with John Forester, David C. Perry, Helen Liggett, Grant Kestor, Milton and Ann Lower, and many others. The practical inspiration has come from my work in the early days of the Blackland Neighborhood Association in Austin, TX and, especially, with the Greater Mankato Area Coalition for Affordable Housing in Mankato, MN. Claire Wilson's editorial assistance was especially helpful.

The information and views contained here are my own or the authors and do not necessarily reflect any views or policies of the U.S. Deptartment of Housing and Urban Development.

This project has received substantial support from the Institute for Advanced Cultural Studies through its director, Robert Merrill.

Dennis G. Crow
Washington, D.C.
March 1990

The Embassy of Canada, 501 Pennsylvania Avenue, Washington, D.C. Building design by Arthur Erikson. Official opening on May 3, 1989. This photo shows the empty or de-centered theme (*see* pp. 112, 155, and 167 below).

Introduction to

Philosophical

Streets

Dennis Crow, AICP

U.S. Dept. of Housing and Urban Development

> The world of concrete personal experiences to which the street belongs is multitudinous beyond imagination, tangled, muddy, painful, and perplexed. The world to which your philosophy professor introduces you is simple, clean, noble. The contradictions of real life are absent from it. Its architecture is classic. Principles of reason trace out its outlines, logical necessities cement its parts. Purity and dignity are what it most expresses. It is a kind of marble temple shining on a hill.
>
> —William James

THE PURPOSE OF THIS BOOK is to challenge architects and planners to re-examine their relationship to both planning theory and contemporary developments in the humanities. Furthermore, its purpose is to challenge scholars in the humanities to bring criticism to bear on the problems of towns, cities, and regions where they live. Many planners, architects, philosophers, and literary critics have attempted to apply hermeneutics, critical theory, poststructuralism, and postmodernism in urban analysis. Their works have ranged from articles and books to conferences, exhibitions, and competitions. Citations from the works of Heidegger, Habermas, Baudrillard, Derrida, and Foucault have appeared in numerous articles on urban form and theory and, according to some architectural critics, in buildings themselves.[1] *Philosophical Streets* will demonstrate in some crucial detail the coincidence in space and time of a new geography of urban disciplines that involves architecture, urban planning, public administration, comparative literature, and philosophy.

William James' comment at the beginning of this introduction illustrates a predisposition in philosophy and the social sciences to oppose philosophy and urbanism in both theory and practice. The current construction of urban academic and professional disciplines implies that philosophy and urbanism are opposed in theory because urbanism is understood as an empirical, quantitative, and practical discipline while philosophy is understood as largely a deductive, conceptual, and academic discipline. However, this contrast can no longer stand in strict opposition within either discipline. Ironically, after decades in which architecture and planning have become exclusively "modern" professions applying engineering and management techniques to social problems, the extensive debates about "critical theory" and "postmodernism" have renewed interest in the philosophical analysis of their theory and practice. The contrast between philosophy and the street is, therefore, much more complicated than James' view expressed above. Through the examples below drawn from urban analysis and literary criticism, I have tried to illustrate that the "street" or the "city" is not necessarily comprehended by empirical description or by social science style "explanation." Similarly "philosophy" is not necessarily confined to the space of theory, no place, or reducible to its application to the city through social science. This introduction and the essays that follow contribute to a new approach to "urbanism" that is as well informed about contemporary philosophy as about the "nuts and bolts" of planning and architectural practice applied to the street.

Jameson (1984), Habermas (1985), Forester (1985), Soja (1989), Harvey (1989), and Beauregard (1989) have published works specifically addressing the relationships between philosophy and urbanism. The essays in *Philosophical Streets* are dedicated to demonstrating that criticism in philosophy and urbanism undermines James' distinction. Furthermore, this introduction appeals to, and the essays illustrate, the ways in which critical theory can be used to renew the relevance of the humanities to urban affairs—and urban affairs to the humanities. The greater challenge is to encourage scholars and students to bring the excitement of theory to the needs of communities where they work and live.

Criticizing applications of contemporary philosophy recently, Peter Hall (1989) has claimed that the adaptation of contemporary French and

German philosophy to urban issues has led to irrelevant theorizing and the neglect of serious urban problems. The ultimate fear that many urban scholars may have is that these contemporary theorists and their allies seem determined to undermine the philosophical, political, and practical foundations that have defined planning and modern architectural practice. Though Hall's analysis is ultimately contradicted by his assumptions about language, reference, and narrative that bring their own metaphysics to his argument, there are more serious limitations to trends in the application of contemporary theory.

First, at a philosophical level, contemporary theorists do fundamentally challenge the putative grounding of philosophical modernism that has guided planning and architectural practice for the last two centuries. Gideon (1963), Boyer (1983), Berman (1982), Benevolo (1971), Hoch (1984), Soja (1989), and many others have written histories of architecture and planning in relation to the history of modern philosophy in its deductive and empiricist varieties. However, new philosophical works challenge assumptions about the logic, concepts, validity, reliability, value-neutrality, and relevance to contemporary urban problems of philosophical modernism that prescribed the search for and application of knowledge that might solve social problems. Through their qualified defense or stark criticism of philosophical modernism, Habermas, Foucault, Derrida, Baudrillard, and others do not offer the prescriptions that have seemingly grounded planning and architecture in the past. Rather, these new works seem to discredit planners' searches for solutions to urban problems as only ruses for increased social control.

Second, on a political level, as a consequence of exposing the short and twisted roots of planning and modern architecture, Habermas, Adorno, Derrida, Foucault, and Baudrillard seem to offer only changes in the ways theorists—but not necessarily practitioners or citizens—talk about planning or offer only justifications for "micrological" political action at the local level.[2] Even if the latter were the implied proper political action, it does not measure up to the technological promise of the 1939 World's Fair, the sweep of "slum clearance" under the federal Urban Renewal program in the 1950's or the vision of the "War on Poverty" and the Model Cities programs in the 1960's, which may be examples of the vision implied still by debates about the lost vision of planning. The implied politics of contemporary theory seem to leave millions of people homeless, hungry, ill, and illiterate and millions more potentially so while theorists write about the miniaturization of circuits of domination, the failure of modern architecture, and the pleasures of aesthetic fragmentation in postmodern culture.

Third, at a practical level, contemporary theory seems to replace the rigor of social science with the subjectivism of aesthetics. To Hall and other scholars in the humanities, the endless analysis of "meaning" has replaced the grasp of "facts." To them, without "facts" there appears to be no continuity between the understanding of urban problems, the selection among alternative solutions, and the policy-making process— that is, there can be no planning at all. If contemporary theory did in fact result in this, perhaps the most extreme, and nevertheless most practical, solution would be to turn the search for "meaning" into the analysis of the historical texts of architecture and planning and turn their rematerialization into the design of mixed-use developments that have no more relationship to urban problems than do the subjective pleasures of affluent people who shop there.

Paradoxically, the contemporary theorists' strength is their challenge to the pretensions of theory in general. Philosophically, their criticism of philosophical modernism warns planners and architects that there is no technological fix to problems of urban environmental pollution, congestion, and the uneven development of urban economies. Furthermore, these contemporary theorists are interested in long-term consequences of problems and are wary of unreflective proposals to solve them. Passionately interested in the potential political consequences of theory and personally aware of the consequences of fascist and colonial domination, these theorists are not quick to endorse appealing political or technical solutions of social scientists, which are still no more than another philosophical genre with meanings enforced by administrative personnel (Crow 1989).

Theoretically, Habermas, Adorno, Foucault, Derrida, and others have argued—in radically different ways—that the dependency of planning on the political process is epistemologically unavoidable, not just practically expedient. Practically, their reintroduction of cultural analysis in planning, urban design in architecture, and urban issues into the humanities broadens professional conceptions of how people experience cities. Forester (1983) argues that the challenge of cultural analysis to the predominant applied social science in planning is an "immense professional and intellectual opportunity." Besides expanding the professional boundaries, it broadens the conception of an individual's experience in cities beyond that of a "rational economic actor," "taxpayer," "underclass" dependent, or homeless "client." Furthermore, as all the authors here attempt to show, the concern in this anthology for cultural analysis crosses the boundaries of the academic disciplines of planning, architecture, philosophy, and comparative literature. Perhaps that concern should improve both the philosophical analysis of planning and the empirical analysis of the urban setting of putative aesthetic objects such as buildings, cities, or what Adorno (1984) called the "culturescape" in general. In short, more theoretical analysis, rather than less, coupled with empirical analysis is needed to remove barriers to citizen participation in policy-making, to break down stereotypes of homeless people and the assistance they need, and to examine the long-term global consequences of uneven development.

1. Examples

The links between theoretical and empirical analyses applied to an "aesthetic" issue can be illustrated through the following example. In several cities across the country, municipal governments have approved specific regulations for the aesthetic appearance of new office buildings. The point of these regulations was to provide incentives for pitched and geometrically ornate roofs. Seattle and San Francisco have recently received publicity for developing ordinances that offer density bonuses for such roofs (Lassar 1989). In Seattle, for example, the Washington Mutual Tower, completed in 1988, was designed by the trendy firm of Kohn Pederson Fox with Venetian gold granite and ornaments to mirror its art deco context. Lassar reports that the tower's developer submitted more than a dozen rooftop designs before receiving a 45,000 square feet bonus from the city. This means that the developer could increase the net rentable space in building by this much floor space (and thereby increase his profits) for adding an acceptably designed roofline. In a *Seattle Post Intelligencer* article, the developer acknowledged that the design was "chosen primarily for aesthetic reasons rather than bonus value" (Lassar 1989). In San Francisco, the 1985 Downtown Plan calls for "thinner . . . more finely detailed buildings" that taper at both ends. In order to "create a new sculptured skyline, new buildings must have generally thinner and more complex shapes." The bonus involved adding ten percent to the height allowed by the existing zoning regulations in exchange for a reduction in the floor area of the upper stories. Such a bonus would in effect compensate the developer for any loss of net rentable space required to meet the design ordinance.

From a strictly functional point of view, the tapering of buildings' upper stories would increase the amount of sunlight on the street and reduce the ground level velocity of the wind created by tall buildings. However, tapering buildings at the lower end actually increases the wind velocity on the sidewalk. From an aesthetic point of view, the result should be to create a "more slender profile and sculptured building termination." Lassar reports very interesting developments in this conjunction of aesthetics and zoning regulations in several cities. Her description of the vocabulary and effect of these ordinances invites several responses. This isolated issue of roof-top design and architecture raises questions about the economic development of urban areas, the politics of urban development, and the relationship between architectural decisions and problems of representation in general, not to mention the psychoanalytic implications. All three of those larger issues are examined throughout the essays in this book.

First, an analysis that begins from problems of urban economic development would conclude that such ordinances create buildings that would attract and fill the offices with corporate headquarters. Those corporate headquarters offices would attract additional well-paid employees to the downtown, invite relatively affluent consumers from other parts of the city and region, and attract other developers and additional buildings. Contrary to the expectations implied by the San Francisco and Seattle ordinances and the economic development analysis, however, Joel Goldsteen argues that aesthetics has no impact on economics. In a quantitative analysis to measure the economic effectiveness of design decisions in Dallas, Goldsteen (1989: 5) found that among variables related to design and aesthetics only landscaping and open space had strong correlations with the occupancy rates of office buildings examined in the Dallas-Ft. Worth metroplex. He concludes that ". . . no architectural or building design element has statistical correlations indicating any strong influence on occupancies." The crucial determinants of "renting-up" office space are access to major arterial streets and freeways and plenty of well-landscaped open space. Even though this case study may not be representative, it does point to the importance of understanding how aesthetics contributes to or does not contribute to the economic success of buildings and urban areas.

Second, the existing and prospective ordinances that Lassar describes arose in the political context of municipal governments' attempts to stimulate economic development. In recent years, public and private plans for the "revitalization" of downtown and inner city areas have included attention to design as well as profitability. In New York, Houston, Minneapolis, Dallas, Detroit, and Los Angeles development corporations and architectural firms lead the way in making "postmodernism" visible and concrete. However, postmodern architecture must pay its bills by accommodating the needs of the corporate headquarters it houses. Those needs are physical, geographic, and aesthetic. Providing for those needs is increasingly a matter of negotiation among architectural firms, development corporations, banks, and municipal governments. Inside municipal governments, providing infrastructural improvements such as streets and sewers is the responsibility of public works departments, reviewing development proposals for compliance with existing zoning and building codes is the responsibility of site review planners, obtaining tax abatements, lower interest loans, state or federal grants, or loan guarantees is the responsibility of financial and planning departments, and final approval of all of this is the responsibility of planning commissions, zoning boards, and city councils. The development of postmodern architecture has not taken place without involving the administrative and political process of municipal and state governments as well as neighborhood groups and community development corporations.

Third, the vocabulary used to describe aesthetic qualities in the examples above points to the language of fashion, popular culture, and, from there, to the realm of postmodern aesthetics. The words "taller," "thinner," and "slender" are like fashion statements for countless commodities and point to the exploitation of women through the codes of fashion. Postmodern architecture is the conjunction of economics and aesthetics and symbolizes their global proportions. In his many recent works, Fredric Jameson (1984, 1985, 1988) has attempted to describe this conjunction and its range from painting to architecture. Edward Soja

(1989) has presented the relationship between architecture, planning, and critical theory in a well written, accurate, and impressive way. I will comment briefly later on the importance of these scholars' work, but they are only two of the scholars trying to bring critical theory to bear on the theoretical and practical problems of architecture and planning.

2. From Urbanism to Criticism

The critical analysis of the distance between the discipline of urban planning and any philosophical questions concerning its epistemological foundation, the relationship of theory to practice, and the relationship of urban planning to other academic and professional disciplines has been episodic and short-lived. Tension between the comprehension of planning as a discipline related to engineering, a model for rigorous social problem-solving, and to the arts, as planning's creative but impractical inspiration, has existed since the nineteenth century. In order to provide a more detailed context for reconsidering this tension, I will present a short story about the representation of the history of planning.

There are many origins of urban planning (Benevolo 1971, Boyer 1983, Hoch 1984, Kreukeburg 1983). The City Beautiful movement, sanitation reform, housing reform, and the rationalization of industrial capitalism all compete for emphasis in stories of the beginnings of urban planning in the U.S. in the nineteenth century. Regardless of its origin, academics and practitioners of urban planning primarily understand it as an empirical, quantitative, and technical discipline. Charles Hoch (1984) has argued that despite ignoring such philosophical issues concerning its grounding and history urban planning theory and practice embody the promise and contradictions of pragmatism. The disciplinary inter-pretation within urban planning holds that it is composed of the empirical analysis of land and real estate economics, transportation patterns, site planning for individual buildings, environmental impacts, population and housing demographics, and the quantitative projection of the results of all these forces. However, the construction of this opposition between the street and philosophy can only be sustained if one assumes that the street is only an empirically describable mélange of events to which theory could make no contribution except as an "explanation" of them and a rationale for controlling them.

Illustrating the construction of this opposition, Boyer (1983: 69) quotes Fredric Law Olmstead Jr.'s definition of urban planning from 1911. Comprehensive urban planning, he suggested,

> is concerned with a single complex subject . . . the intelligent control and guidance of the entire physical growth and alteration of cities; embracing all the problems of transportation facilities or of recreation facilities, congestion in respect to the means of supplying light, air, water, or anything else essential to the health and happiness of the people.

The theory and practice of urban planning in the U.S. have not evolved far from this broad definition, even if the favored methodologies for analysis and action have switched from architecture and civil engineering to social science and economics. Planners are trained in quantitative social sciences, economics, and the methods and problems of their specialization, e.g., land-use regulation and zoning, transportation, or economic development. Using these skills, planners may plan streets, sewer lines, or downtown revitalization efforts, issue building permits, recommend zoning changes, or administer housing programs for lower income or homeless persons. Over the years, planning practice has changed to acknowledge and expand the participation of citizens in the regulatory and planning processes. Furthermore, there is a great deal of discussion about the relationship between planning processes and political institutions as well as about the politics of planning practice itself.

Despite the persistence of many borders of the discipline, the views of scholars and practitioners about the contribution of philosophy varies from having no useful contribution to being the conscience of planning practice. Nevertheless, for ideological and practical reasons—which Forester (1983, 1985) and Boyer (1983) outline—the discipline has lost its visible and active relationship to philosophical and aesthetic modernism. Given the strong arguments of Marcuse, Adorno, Habermas, Foucault, Derrida, Lyotard, Baudrillard, and many other scholars—however allied with these—planning theorists have been attracted to seemingly generalizable concepts borrowed from the humanities such as "sign," "text," "discourse," or "communication" in their analysis of the relationship of planning practice and politics. Similarly, in order to interpret the relationships of literature and art to politics and power, scholars in the humanities have turned to similar sources.[3] The work of John Forester (1985) in urban and regional planning and public administration has been exemplarily in this regard.[4] Drawing extensively on Habermas' work, Forester has attempted to synthesize, apply, and communicate to general audiences the importance of issues of meaning and power to the theory and practice of urban planning. Charles Hoch (1988) and M. Christine Boyer (in this volume) have also written on the relationship of the work of Foucault and Habermas to urban planning.

Given his research in critical theory, broadly interpreted, Forester is interested in the legitimation of power through the theoretical works and professional routines of planning practice. He has succeeded in making it applicable to the practical concerns of the planning profession. In his introduction to *Critical Theory and Public Life*, Forester (1985: xvi) summarizes the political purpose of his and others' use of Habermas' work. These social science scholars are "concerned not with the realization of an ideal speech situation but with specific problems of power and powerlessness, with ideology, legitimation, and democratic politics. They are concerned with social research efforts that will enable practical analyses of—and political responses to—operative, systematic distortions of everyday communicative interactions."

In a small salient piece on current changes in the disciplines, Forester broadens his analysis and traces the history of planning's reliance on social science and policy analysis for its models and training. In theory and in practice through federal programs such as Urban Renewal and Model Cities from the 1950's through the mid-1970's, urban planning followed the rise of policy analysis. Forester argues that until recently professional training and practice were to follow the methods and results of policy analysis and apply them to the traditional specializations. However, in the 1980's, the abolition or decline of federal urban programs, the failure of policy analysis to bring about its recommended changes, and the ideological and philosophical criticisms of policy analysis have sapped its power over urban planning. Furthermore, the incorporation of social science into urban planning erased urban planning's historical relationship to architecture and urban design. In practice the separation of planning and design left scores of unattractive, desolate, and, thereby, dangerous buildings and central cities. Forester argues that as a result urban planning is now being challenged by architecture and urban design. He argues that

The opportunity, of course, is that the reintegration of design will provide the occasion for planners to teach and learn from those who have thought about the problems of judgment, in addition to those of calculation, for a long time, particularly from those concerned with the evaluation of action, argument, text, symbol, and meaning, where interpretations still had to be given, defended, justified, and legitimated.

Forester's argument here goes beyond his research in the practices of distorted communication. The concepts and uses of "text, symbol, and meaning" cannot be analyzed through the use of Habermas' work alone. These concepts belong to aesthetics generally which have undergone extensive scrutiny in recent years. Furthermore, the analysis and construction of urban design is beyond the training and practice of most urban planners. Forester's remarks invite the theoretical and practical redefinition of the relationships between urbanism and the humanities.

This challenge to address aesthetic theory comes from both architects and scholars in the humanities. The former are trained in techniques of aesthetic transformation of space and the latter in the interpretation of aesthetic judgment. Architecture encompasses the theory and practice of aesthetic judgment in an art form, and the humanities attempt to comprehend, or deconstruct, the theory and practical implications of aesthetics in general. Responding to this challenge, planning with its theoretical pretensions about comprehensiveness and its practical aspirations to make its theory work can be drawn to both architecture as a practical discipline and the humanities as a body of disparate theoretical ones.

There are several things that scholars in the humanities could contribute to the work of Forester, Boyer, Hoch, and others: (1) more detailed analyses of the philosophical presuppositions in the work of Habermas, Foucault, Adorno, Lyotard, Baudrillard, and Derrida—especially as these authors reveal the ideological content of urban theory; (2) analyses of the differences among these authors' works; (3) analyses of the desirability and plausibility of a critical pragmatist response to Richard Rorty and Lyotard; and (4) expansion of the theoretical and practical scope of urbanists' interests in the real conflicts of gender, race, urban violence, wage discrimination, police brutality, and the international division of labor.

3. From Criticism to Urbanism

Scholars in the humanities (especially, Berman 1982 and Jameson 1984, 1988) have written major works on questions of modernism in the arts and architecture and its relationship to urban issues. In the wake of the economic, spatial, and aesthetic "revitalization" of some central cities, interpreting the meaning of those events, places, and symbols has become an interest of cultural analysts and philosophers. Such questions in literary theory are attracting many scholars in philosophy and the humanities to the analysis of architecture and planning.

Frank Lentricchia has raised similar issues. William James' remark, which serves as a headnote for this introduction, appears in Lentricchia's *Ariel and the Police* to set the stage for a discussion of aesthetics and social science in which he illustrates a curious correlation between their orders and resistance (1988: 105).[5] Lentricchia begins his discussion of James by referring to the contrast between theory, or what I would call the space of theory, and "geography of practices." Lentricchia's combination of terms here implies a relationship between urbanism and criticism. He argues that James is writing against Santayana's "excathedra" style of theorizing in which the space of theory is ideally, Lentricchia says, a place for "becoming nobody" in "no place" in "no time." He goes on to say, "In this serene, epistemologically and morally secure space, beyond ideology, one has knowledge of the real order and value of all things." Lentricchia reminds us that even the early modernist Marxists and pragmatists argued against this sort of "foundationalism." James pejoratively referred to such pretensions of philosophy as "abstract."

Lentricchia contrasts this space of theory—distancing itself from specific places, times, and people—to James' world of the "geography of practices." He argues that in James' "fully articulated pragmatism . . . there is nothing but practice, but the practice carries with it the obligations of revision, that practice tends to force constant scrutiny of one's work in its context" (1988: 108). The context of practice and inquiry for such old pragmatists as James, Pierce, and Dewey is the "situated intellectual involvement with real local effects." In 1897, Dewey argued that knowledge "can define the percept and elaborate the concept, but their unity can be found only in action." Completing his Hegelian history of philosophy—ending in the streets of the United States and not in Prussia—Dewey sees its course in "the growing transfer of interest from metaphysics and the theory of knowledge to psychology and social ethics—including in the latter term all the related concrete social sciences, so far as they can give guidance to conduct." Lentricchia notes that for James rationalists would make all texts on the universe correspond, in James' words, to "the one real one, the infinite folio, or *edition de luxe*." Lentricchia (1988: 111) follows James' textual metaphor further and suggests that James instead "speaks for the liberation of the small, the regional, the locally embedded, the underdog: the voice that refuses the elocutionary lessons of cosmopolitan finishing schools."[6]

The point here is not to defend the old or new pragmatists, but to illustrate a traditional opposition between theory and practice that haunts the disciplines of urban planning and the humanities. Writing inside philosophy, James argues against the universalizing pretensions of theory and its supposed practice as academic "professional" philosophy. The old pragmatists argued for the applicability of philosophy to social, local, and specifically, urban problems.[7] However, in their criticism of philosophy as "abstract" and "cosmopolitan," the pragmatists seem to have invited, or even legitimated, the rejection of philosophy altogether in favor of applied social science.

Lentricchia sets his careful reading of the old pragmatism and his criticism of the politics of the new pragmatism within a book about Wallace Stevens. Because of Stevens' dual life of technical bureaucratic work and of poetry, Lentricchia (1988: 26) writes that he "inhabits the world of James and Foucault, he is wary of system and surveillance and of the police in all the contemporary and protean guises." I am tempted to interpret Lentricchia's book as the disclosure of Stevens' own relationship to philosophy and the streets he roamed in search of tea and chocolate, for it is about this as much as it is about the relationship between the humanities and the applied social sciences, particularly urban planning.

In addition, Fredric Jameson has written extensively about the relationship between architectural "postmodernism" and its significance in popular culture and for the quality of urban life.[8] His essay, "Postmodernism, or the Cultural Logic of Late Capitalism," highlights Jameson's interest in architecture. He describes the connection between critical theory and architecture—as both an academic discipline and a profession—in the following comments from various places in the essay:

> Architecture is . . . of all the arts that closest to the economic,
> with which, in the form of commissions and land values, it has
> a virtually unmediated relationship; it will therefore not be sur-
> prising to find the extraordinary flowering of the new postmodern
> architecture grounded in the patronage of multinational businesses
> whose expansion and development is strictly contemporaneous
> with it. . . . Architecture therefore remains . . . the privileged
> aesthetic language; and the distorting and fragmenting reflections
> of one enormous glass surface or the other can be taken as para-
> digmatic of the central role of process and reproduction in post-
> modern culture.

Though his major concern is the interpretation of the cultural significance
of postmodernism, he is careful to analyze its relationship to the "real"
economic events that give cities around the world their appearance. Such
comments on architecture and cities are rare among scholars in the humanities. Nevertheless, these specific comments are limited by a view that
sees single buildings as the focal point of urban development and as
"virtually unmediated" by politics and administration. Though Jameson
has done much to put architecture and urbanism back on the map of
the humanities, his analysis needs the teamwork of people familiar with
the broader ranges of the practice of urban development.

More recently, Jameson has expanded the scope of his work to include
the concept of "space" generally. His latest work encompasses the concerns
for urban design and implicitly of urban economics. The following comment
summarizes those concerns (1988: 351):

> You should understand that I take such spatial peculiarities of
> postmodernism as symptoms and expression of a new and
> historically original dilemma, one that involves our insertion as
> individual subjects into a multidimensional set of radically dis-
> continuous realities, whose frames range from the still surviving
> spaces of bourgeois private life all the way to the unimaginable
> decentering of global capital itself. . . . And although you may
> not have realized it, I am talking about practical politics here:
> since the crisis of socialist internationalism, and the enormous
> strategic and tactical difficulties of coordinating local and grass-

roots or neighhorhood political actions with national or international
ones, such urgent political dilemmas are all immediately functions
of the enormously complex new international space I have in mind.

In this one comment, Jameson touches on many of the theoretical and
political concerns common to urbanists and humanists. Though there
are critical and political interests that the individual scholars may have
in common, sharing concepts, data, and political commitments across
the disciplines is not easy. Humanists' concern for interpretation of
modernism requires more than borrowing seemingly generalizable concepts
from social science such as "modernization," "class," "multinational
corporations," or "late capitalism." These concepts are too vague to
provide insight into the complexity of urban economies around the world.
Three things are needed to develop Jameson's (and other literary critics')
analysis: (1) the introduction of the study of the role of urban planning
and the technical and political constraints it places on urban development;
(2) the use of more sophisticated theories of global urban economics;
and (3) the analysis of the rhetorical conduct and narratives from which
those economic theories are constructed.

What might a more sophistocated critical analysis look like? Combining
a detailed history of modern art and the history of urban development,
Marshall Berman (1982) has written a very exciting work on modernism
in the humanities and its relationship to the transformation of the Bronx.
His work contains many detailed analyses of art and literature, but for
my purpose here I would mention two of his summary comments. Taking
"modernism" as more than a conceptual apparatus defining art and
architecture, Berman (1982: 345-346) summarizes what modernism in
art and cities have in common: "To be modern . . . is to experience
personal and social life as a maelstrom, to find one's world and oneself
in perpetual disintegration and renewal, trouble and anguish, ambiguity
and contradiction: to be part of a universe in which all that is solid melts
into air. To be modernist is to make oneself somehow at home in the
maelstrom. . . ." The "maelstrom" is the construction and demolition
of art forms and cities as well. The "modernization" process is the reproduction of capitalism made locally visible through the public and private
sector actions of urban development and through the patterns of housing,
transportation, and sanitation it creates.[9] These cultural events and urban
patterns are perhaps only analogous, but their proximity in New York,

Paris, Los Angeles, or Vienna makes persuasive their characterization as metonymic. Their combination is personal and local because people live in cities where they are visible in greater proportions than in other places such as rural areas and because people continue to live with the unpredictable effects of both the aesthetic and economic processes.

Such reflections of events facilitate Berman's (1982: 345) following comment: "I could go on talking about more exciting modernist works of the past decade. Instead, I thought to end up with the Bronx, with an encounter with some ghosts of my own." He writes as though this were an unusually subjective ending to a properly scholarly work, a conclusion that signifies a personal emotion that drives the book. Even though this comment works that way rhetorically, it is not a strictly personal or subjective statement. The actions of Robert Moses, the untrained "expert" and unelected political leader who most shaped New York, and the action or lack of action by other planners and developers that shaped the Bronx were bigger than almost anywhere else in the U.S. Berman rebuilds the discursive, practical, geographic, and personal ties between philosophy and the street that James saw being turned into the walls of an academic discipline. Berman's attention to the Bronx is important to him and to the history of urban planning because of the scale of Moses' "meat-axe" of destruction. However, its scale should not deceive Berman, Jameson, or Soja into arguing that New York or Los Angeles represent unique cases. The temporal and spatial relationships of culture and urban development, for example, are as important and complex for the people from Mexico or Laos who live in Wells, Minnesota, as for those who live in New York or Los Angeles (Crow 1987). The cultural and economic scale and locality of this "modernism" across the globe should be explored. Such shared theoretical and practical interests of critical social theorists in the humanities and urbanism yield the advice that the "local" should be a disputed concept as well as the "global" and the "universal."

4. Criticism and Community Development

The argument outlined here is not a simple naive appeal to be more careful about our terms, but is an appeal to use what we know about the specifics of the putative objects of both disciplines, "cities" and "texts," at every turn. Scholars in planning, architecture, and the humanities have a great deal yet to learn from each of these disciplines. Merely exchanging vocabularies creates more debt on the account of each discipline. Each discipline needs more critical empirical and theoretical work rather than less. I would be the last to call for an uncritical convergence of topics and analysis. The authors selected for this book have demonstrated both their knowledge of details of urban problems and planning as well as the details of cultural analysis. They have managed to weave both together in exciting ways. Their works are good examples of how this can be done in a scholarly and politically critical way. The authors' arguments are shaped by the coincidental point at which the disciplines are made more complex by the increasingly complex physical and economic geography of cities where they practice them.

"Space," both disciplinary and economic, is a useful concept to measure the uneven terrain of the disciplines and to reflect on the possible causes and legitimating institutions of the changing distribution of capital. This concept or metaphor is calling urbanists and humanists together. Paradoxically, "space" is not a place, but it can only be interpreted in the relationships among places. Similarly, its interpretation is not the domain of a particular discipline, but is the interaction of scholars among the humanities and urban professions. Just as the relationships between local and global economies are becoming more visible through complex interpretation, the relationships between the disciplines are as well.

The "grammatological 'space'" (Ulmer 1985) opened up by Derrida's work makes topics of geometry, architecture, and design intriguing to scholars in the humanities. Derrida's work shows in so many ways how architecture has always surrounded philosophy and thereby raises the curtain that has divided academic and professional disciplines. The practice of border crossing or curtain raising is perhaps the analogical antonym of architectural practice; deconstruction and philosophy are irreducible disciplines, but the concepts of figure, analogy, metonymy, metaphor, catachresis, and so on that might be used to describe those relationships are also subject to analysis. In the interview with Christopher Norris, Derrida (1988: 8) remarks, "Of course there is a lot of architectural metaphor, not only in my texts, but in the whole philosophical tradition. And deconstruction—the word 'Deconstruction'—sounds very much like such a metaphor, an architectural metaphor. . . . But deconstruction doesn't mean that we have to stay within those architectural metaphors. . . .

Deconstruction is perhaps a way of questioning the architectural model itself." In these comments on architecture, Derrida goes on transporting all his material on the concept/metaphor problematic. Perhaps, however, there is a more solid joint between criticism and urbanism.

This border crossing, this craft of joining, is not confined to the stylizing of buildings or criticism. Mapping the boundaries of architecture and criticism is confounded on one border by the theoretical analysis of economic geography—in all its styles of analysis from central place theory to post-Marxist dependency theory—and on the other border by the "real" facts of unemployment, homelessness, hunger, ecological destruction, and demographic change. In the former realm, "space" is no place confined exclusively by the inventions of longitude and latitude, but is a feature of the mode of production (Gottdeiner 1985). In the other region, people live out the physical and emotional consequences of actions taken in the other. The academic and professional practioners of the disciplines of criticism, design, planning, and political economy inhabit these regions behind their curtains of self-declared independence at their peril. Moreover, any successful attempt to merge them would jeopardize their separate potential for social change that makes them attractive in the first instance.

Since the authors presented here draw theoretical assistance mainly from "poststructuralism," interpreting the political significance of this approach is particularly important. Though Adorno's style and analysis have a poststructuralist edge, his political concerns and criticism are more direct and well known. While the politics of poststructuralism has been subject to tremendous misunderstanding, Radhakrishnan (1989) presents one of the best interpretations. Even though I am unjustly simplifying his argument, there are four points that could guide an interpretation of the political significance of the essays here.

Radhakrishnan first argues that poststructuralist politics exhibits a "single-minded resistance to 'authority' and official accommodation." One task of Derridean deconstruction is to interrogate the semantic and syntactic features of texts as well as classifications, examples, citations, translations, graphics, etc. that often present themselves as the unimpeachable authority of political, administrative, and planning decisions. In "Authority and Administration" (Crow 1989) and in "Le Corbusier's Post-Modern Plan" (this volume), I attempt to show that such criticism challenges, but neither could nor should destroy, administrative authority. Radhakrishnan's point is to question the authority of canonical texts and political documents as the starting point of a poststructuralist politics.

Next Radhakrishnan argues that poststructuralist politics interrogates the "ratio of the interplay between 'identity' and 'difference.'" Derrida's analysis of the epistemological instability of philosophical authority leads to an analysis of the self-proclaimed "center" of Western philosophy, its "margins" and the concepts of "identity," "difference," and "totality" which philosophers have used to maintain that stability. Our dependence on the presumed certainty, centrality, and clarity of concepts like "foundation," "subject," "object," "truth," "fact," and so on makes any challenge to them seem to lead to perpetual analysis and political paralysis. The concepts of the "identity" and "difference" necessarily cannot be presumed to refer absolutely to any object of analysis and can only be provisionally applied in the attempt to comprehend action taken by individuals, groups, or classes. Determining what bearing, if any, this has on objects or individual's "existence" or "reality" is a philosophical issue itself subject to revision. The construction of ratios of putative identity and difference for any object of analysis, individual, gender, or class, is a quintessentially political gesture—to identify a proper political agent. Poststructuralist political analyses concern the ways in which politicians and administrators do or might use theoretical and practical assumptions about individuals, groups, and classes to disable or enable political action. Though Radhakrishnan's focus is limited to electoral politics, the analysis of the "ratio of the interplay between 'identity' and 'difference'" might well be extended to political and planning texts, to actual or proposed "communities," to interpretations of the course of local economic development, to the "state," and to philosophy itself.

The third point follows from this and is that political analysis and action must proceed from choice: a choice for a philosophically and empirically scrutinized ratio of "identity" and "difference." The choice is, at the very least, for political (and, by implication, administrative and economic) authority that does not declare its own certainty, universality, and univocality through official documents or theory. Poststructuralist politics is the interrogation of the legitimation of authority; furthermore, it applies its analysis recursively to concepts, models, and ideologies that people provisionally use to legitimate and guide political action.

The fourth point is that recursive criticism leads to political paralysis for the isolated individual theorist or political activist who is waiting for the individual, group, or class to appear and act in a way that mirrors the "correct" theoretical "subject-position." In Radhakrishnan's works, such a recursive poststructuralist politics "is appropriate and valid not because theory says or wills so in abeyance of reality, but rather because such a politics is already afoot." The poststructuralist political practice that precedes theory is the coalitional politics of marginalized, largely urban, populations who work together in such activities as electoral politics, neighborhood revitalization, and human services provision. Though Radhakrishnan and other theorists have singled out Jesse Jackson's "Rainbow Coalition" as the exemplary political practice, there are many other coalitions that

> cut across and defy 'given' boundaries and properties such as race, gender, sexuality, ethnicity, economic and academic status, class, etc. . . . There is no axiomatic one to one correspondence between the political ethic of any one of the components of the rainbow and that of the rainbow as such. Values, valences, and priorities are established as part of an ongoing negotiation where the regional interests of a particular group within the coalition are read in terms of the other interests that make up the ever expanding rainbow. . . . The delicate task is to produce a double reading that in enfranchising the right of one group will not deny the connectedness of that group to the other groups.
> (Radhakrishnan 1989: 326)

Radhakrishnan provides an accurate account of theoretical poststructuralist politics. His point is quite simple: the "identity" of the "agent" of political action is negotiated through the action of shifting coalitions. Even though Radhakrishnan attempts to comprehend urban political coalitions in a new way, he has not undone the old interpretation of the role of self-interest as the primary motivation in coalition building. Though comparing his interpretation with standard theories of coalition building is an important research task, there is a more important philosophical point implied by his analysis. By suggesting that the practice of the Rainbow Coalition precedes any attempt to theoretically interpret it, Radhakrishnan cleverly suggests that practice precedes theory and that theorists' attempts to comprehend it cannot keep up. Furthermore, recognizing this, a poststructuralist politics would recognize that its theory cannot undo previous approaches to political change or create new ones *ad hoc* on the basis of theory alone and without acknowledging existing and developing political, administrative, and social approaches to social justice.

Radhakrishnan implies that the standard interpretation that the primary importance of political theory is to ground and guide practice should be questioned as well. As Radhakrishnan implies, the "progressive" coalition building practiced throughout the 1970's is still with us and cannot be undone so quickly by theory alone. Advocacy by urban and rural coalitions to change political and administrative practice is still viable. The political implication of "philosophical streets" is that engagement for use and resistance with street-level bureaucracy is more important than ever to the life of theory and the practice of social change. In many ways the complexity of the street cannot be matched through theory and theory cannot be readily translated into practice. Arguments can be made that this asymmetry of theory and practice is a strength. Furthermore, the more that the adequacy of theory to map political and administrative practice can be challenged, perhaps the more relevant theory can become if the drive towards total comprehension is overpowered by the need to understand local and regional political practice.

Much more could be said about Radhakrishnan's own and others' practices of political theorizing, but the relevance of his point for *Philosophical Streets* needs elaboration. Though the authors here may not directly state the political significance of their analyses, their analyses point to the politics Radhakrishnan outlines. However, the limitations and opportunities for thought and action are much greater than he states. First, though theorists' attention to the "Rainbow Coalition," which probably has a different identity in Chicago, Los Angeles, New York, Philadelphia, and Washington, D.C., is short-sighted, it points to the expansion of old coalitions based soley on political parties and labor organizations. Second, though the focus of critical theorists seems confined still to the empirical demonstrations of a coalition's viability in urban electoral politics, their theoretical contribution requires the deconstruction of the oppositions of politics and administration or politics and planning and the analysis of coalitions formed to address housing, income, health, and environmental issues in non-electoral advocacy and service delivery actions. Such coalitions formed to practice community development and neighborhood service delivery challenge the boundaries of existing institutions. Third, as the essays collected here illustrate, careful criticism of the disciplinary boundaries might provide an intrinsic rationale for the collaboration between university personnel and such professional, political, or service coalitions. Fourth, poststructuralist analysis, combined in particular with political-economy and traditional planning analysis, can inspire analysis of those oppositions of local *vs* global or rural *vs* urban that limit interpretation of practices that still exceed the grasp of theory.

In the late nineteenth century, William James read about homeless families in New York and Cleveland and criticized philosophical rationalism and idealism for theorizing them out of existence. Today we are still reading about homeless families, but the criticism in contemporary escapist philosophizing often leaves us dazzled by its expanse, subtlety, and brilliance—often because of its strong oppositional posture. Criticism can now address urban issues head-on but should not be the mirror into which critics gaze and should not take on the character of urban entertainment as have the cities and events being criticized. An uncritical return to philosophical modernism is not called for because, as the essays here illustrate, its claims to describe empirically and resolve scientifically urban problems only further mask urban problems once again. Perhaps what we can learn is a vigilance to the practical details that necessarily elude theory, however sophisticated, and to the specificity of theories that might perhaps spur coalitions of theorists and enable their practice and that of others.

Future Works

Philosophical Streets is the first book in the Urbs et Orbis series sponsored by the Institute for Advanced Cultural Studies and Maisonneuve Press. The purpose of the series is to publish works related to the issues above and to provide new opportunities for scholars in urban studies and the humanities to learn of each other's work. We hope to go beyond debates about postmodernism and the appropriation of scholarship from the humanities to a wider range of analysis. The Institute will publish both empirical and theoretical work which emphasizes regional economic and cultural differentiation, the theoretical specificity and differences of interdisciplinary scholars, the exploration of disciplinary redefinition, and the reinterpretation of modernism and postmodernism and the limits of both concepts. The quantity of scholarship in these areas demonstrates that there is academic interest in both the humanities and urban studies. If that interest is to become a viable part of interdisciplinary scholarship, that quantity must be matched by quality. Young scholars trained to read the nuances of theory and practice have much to contribute to this effort.

Notes

1. The related literature in architecture and planning alone grows daily. Forester (1985), Harvey (1987), and Soja (1989) present some of the best collections and arguments. Habermas (1985) and Derrida (1989) have commented on the relevance of their work for architecture and planning. Derrida is particularly circumspect about the appropriation of "deconstruction" under the rubric of "deconstructivist architecture," the subject of a study by Norris and Benjamin (1988). Papadakis (1987, 1989) and Johnson and Wigley (1988) have edited anthologies on this controversy. Perhaps the wildest collection is the volumes of *Zone* edited by Feher and Kwinter (1986).

2. According to Peter Hall, John Forester's work with Habermas' version of critical theory leads to nothing more than "advocacy planning" which Hall seems to assume is merely advocacy at the neighborhood level for lower income people. Hall does acknowledge Hoch's research and personal involvement in helping homeless people in Chicago, but does not connect this with Hoch's theoretical work on Dewey and Foucault. Charles Hoch, Howell Baum, Seymour Mandelbaum, and Floyd Lapp respond to Hall's views in "Letters to the Editor," *Journal of the American Planning Association*, 56, 1 (Winter, 1990): 85-88.

3. The list of works in this area seems to grow daily (Berman 1982; Wallis 1984; Nelson 1986, 1988; Nelson and Grossberg 1988; Arac 1986; Ross 1988; Kellner 1989). A particularly close connection between the disciplinary concerns of English and urban and regional planning occurs in Susan Wells' (1986) work as well as in that of Jennifer Bloomer in this volume.

4. I am neglecting the theoretical connections to be made by scholars in comparative literature, women's studies, and architecture. John Forester, Howell Baum, Charles Hoch, Richard Bolan, Jerome Kaufman, Dennis Crow, and others are part of the Research Group on Planning Practice of the Association of Collegiate Schools of Planning. Members of the research group have done theoretical and empirical research on the relationships of power and meaning in professional planning settings. In addition, similar research has been done by Cynthia McSwain, Bayard Caytron, Michael Harmon, Orion White, and Frank Fisher in Public Administration and by Fred Dallmayr in Political Science. David C. Perry (1987) and Gayatri C. Spivak (1987) continue to make major contributions in political economy. Hardly exhaustive, this note presents major scholars in social science.

5. Quoted in Lentricchia (1988: 113). James' (1981: 14) statement para-phrases a student's thesis about the irreconcilable difference between philosophy and social life. James compares reports on homeless families in Cleveland and New York with the harmonious world contemplated by the Anglo-American Hegelians, Royce and Bradley. He demonstrates how pragmatism overcomes this separation and replaces it with a "turn toward concreteness and adequacy, towards facts, towards action and towards power." Hickman (1990) argues that in Dewey's later work philosophy becomes a criticism of criticism, "a liaison officer between various methods and disciplines, and a 'groundmap of criticism.'"

6. George Santayana (1967: 92) wrote of William James: "There is a sense in which James was not a philosopher at all. . . . Philosophy to him was rather like a maze in which he happened to find himself wandering, and what he was looking for was a way out. In the presence of theories of any sort he was attentive, puzzled, suspicious, with a certain inner prompting to disregard them." Perhaps one should substitute the word "city" for "maze." Perhaps he was looking for a plan, but one of which he would be equally suspicious.

7. Samuel Weber (1987) has written an important essay the relationship between Pierce's work and the rise of social and urban professions. Derrida (1983) follows Weber with an argument on technique, academic disciplines, and the need for vigilance against the instrumental use of academic disciplines.

8. Douglas Kellner (1989) provides an excellent guide to Jameson's work and the bibliography lists Jameson's essays related to architecture and urbanism.

9. An important weakness of Berman's book is his attempt to link "modernism" and "modernization" as co-terminus artistic and economic processes. The scholars in "development theory," especially those frequently noted in the literature available in the U.S., e.g., Samir Amin, André Gundar Frank, A. Emmanuel, David Harvey, Niel Smith, and Ernest Mandel, have roundly criticized the politics and economics of such a comparison. Soja (1989: 109-117) as well as Blomstrom and Hettne (1984) discuss the history and contribution of development theory to refining the theories of urban economics.

References

Adorno, Theodor W. (1984). *Aesthetic Theory*. Trans. C. Lenhardt. Ed. Gretel Adorno and Rolf Tiedeman. London: Routledge and Kegan Paul.

Arac, Jonathan, ed. (1986). *Postmodernism and Politics*. Minneapolis: University of Minnesota Press.

Beauregard, Robert, ed. (1989). *Economic Restructuring and Political Response*. Berkeley: Sage Publications.

Berman, Marshall. (1982). *All That Is Solid Melts Into Air*. New York: Simon and Shuster.

Benevolo, Leonardo. (1971). *The Origins of Modern Town Planning*. Trans. Judith Landry. Cambridge, MA: MIT Press.

Blomstrom, Magnus and Björn Hettne. (1984). *Development Theory in Transition*. London: Zed Books.

Boyer, M. Christine. (1983). *Dreaming the Rational City*. Cambridge: MIT Press.

Crow, Dennis. (1987). *Housing Directions 2000: Wells, Minnesota*. Mankato, MN: Urban and Regional Studies Institute.

————. (1989). "Authority and Administration." Unpublished manuscript.

Derrida, Jacques. (1983). "The Principle of Reason: The University in the Eyes of its Pupils." *Diacritics*, (Fall): 3-20.

————. (1989). "Interviewed by Christopher Norris." *Deconstruction II*. Ed. Andreas C. Papadakis. London: Academe Group, Ltd.

Dewey, John. (1897). "The Significance of the Problem of Knowledge." *University of Chicago Contributions to Philosophy*, 4 (1): 3-20.

Feher, Michel and Sanford Kwinter, eds. (1986). *Zone*. Vols. 1 and 2. Cambridge, MA: MIT Press.

Forester, John. (1983). "The Coming Design Challenge." *Journal of Planning Education and Research*. 3 (Summer): 57-59.

————. (1985). "Introduction: The Applied Turn in Contemporary Critical Theory." *Critical Theory and Public Life*. Ed. John Forester. Cambridge, MA: MIT Press. ix-xix.

Gideon, Sigfried. (1963). *Space, Time, and Architecture: The Growth of a New Tradition*. 4th. Edition. Cambridge, MA: Harvard University Press.

Goldsteen, Joel B. (1989). "What Fills an Office Building? Its Neighborhood or Its Design." *Urban Land*, 48 (4): 2-5.

Gottdeiner, Mark. (1985). *The Social Production of Urban Space*. Austin: University of Texas Press.

Habermas, Jürgen. (1985). "Modern and Postmodern Architecture." *Critical Theory and Public Life*. Ed. J. Forester. Cambridge, MA: MIT Press. 325-329.

Hall, Peter. (1989). "The Turbulent Eighth Decade: Challenges to American City Planning." *Journal of the American Planning Association*, 55 (Summer): 275-282.

Harvey, David. (1987). "Flexible Accumulation through Urbanization: Reflections on 'Postmodernism' in the American City." *Antipode*, 19 (3): 260-286.

————. (1989). *The Condition of Postmodernity: An Essay on the Causes of Cultural Change*. Oxford: Basil Blackwell, Ltd.

Hickman, Larry. (1990). *John Dewey's Pragmatic Technology*. Bloomington: Indiana University Press.

Hoch, Charles. (1984). "Doing Good and Being Right: The Pragmatic Connection in Planning Theory." *Journal of the American Planning Association*, (Summer): 335-345.

————. (1988). "Planning and Pragmatism." *Society*. 26 (Nov.-Dec.): 27-35.

James, William. (1981). *Pragmatism*. Ed. Bruce Kuklick. Indianapolis, IN: Hackett Publishing Co.

Jameson, Fredric. (1984). "Postmodernism, or the Cultural Logic of Late Capitalism. *New Left Review*, 146 (July/Aug.): 53-92.

————. (1985). "Architecture and the Critique of Ideology." *Architecture Criticism Ideology*. Ed. Dimitri Porphirios. Princeton: Princeton Architectural Press. 51-87.

_____. (1988). "Cognitive Mapping." *Marxism and the Interpretation of Culture.* Ed. Cary Nelson and Lawrence Grossberg. Urbana: University of Illinois Press. 347-360.

Johnson, Philip and Mark Wigley, eds. (1988). *Deconstructivist Architecture.* Boston: Little, Brown and Company.

Kellner, Douglas, ed. (1989). *Postmodernism/Jameson/Critique.* Washington, D.C.: Maisonneuve Press.

Kreukeburg, Donald A., ed. (1983). *Introduction to Planning History in the United States.* New Brunswick, NJ: The Center for Urban Policy Research.

Lassar, Terry Jill. (1989). *Carrots & Sticks: New Zoning Downtown.* Washington, D.C.: Urban Land Institute.

Lentricchia, Frank. (1988). *Ariel and the Police.* Madison, WI: University of Wisconsin Press.

Nelson, Cary, ed. (1986). *Theory in the Classroom.* Urbana: Illinois Press.

_____ and Lawrence Grossberg, eds. (1988). *Marxism and the Interpretation of Culture.* Urbana: University of Illinois Press.

Norris, Christopher and Andrew Benjamin. (1988). *What is Deconstruction.* London: St. Martin's Press.

Papadakis, Andreas C. ed. (1987). *Postmodernism and Discontinuity.* London: St. Martin's Press.

_____. (1989). *Deconstruction II.* London: Academe Group, Ltd.

Perry, David C. (1987). "The Politics of Dependency in Deindustrializing America." *The Capitalist City.* Ed. M. P. Smith and J. R. Feagin. London: Basil Blackwell, Ltd.

Radhakrishnan, R. (1989). "Poststructuralist Politics: Towards a Theory of Coalition." *Postmodernism/Jameson/Critique.* Ed. D. Kellner. Washington, D.C.: Maisonneuve Press. 301-332.

Ross, Andrew, ed. (1988). *Universal Abandon.* Minneapolis: University of Minnesota Press.

Santayana, George. (1967). *Character and Opinion in the United States.* New York: W. W. Norton & Company, Inc.

Spivak, Gayatri C. (1987). *In Other Worlds: Essays in Cultural Politics.* London: Methuen.

Soja, Edward W. (1989). *Postmodern Geographies: The Reassertion of Space in Critical Social Theory.* London and New York: Verso Press.

Ulmer, Gregory. (1985). *Applied Grammatology: Post(e)-Pedagogy from Jacques Derrida to Joseph Beuys.* Baltimore: Johns Hopkins University Press.

Weber, Samuel. (1987). "The Limits of Professionalism." *Institution and Interpretation.* Minneapolis: University of Minnesota Press. 18-32.

Wallis, Brian. (1984). *Art After Modernism: Rethinking Representation.* New York: The Museum of Contemporary Art.

Wells, Susan. (1986). "Jurgen Habermas, Communicative Competence, and the Teaching of Technical Discourse." *Theory in the Classroom.* Ed. Cary Nelson. Urbana: University of Illinois Press. 245-269.

Culture

---

and

Administration

Theodor W. Adorno

Trans. by Wes Blomster

WHOEVER SPEAKS of culture speaks about administration as well,[1] whether this is his intention or not. The combination of so many things lacking a common denominator—such as philosophy and religion, science and art, forms of conduct and mores—and finally the inclusion of the objective spirit of an age in the single word "culture" betrays from the outset the administrative view, the task of which, looking down from on high, is to assemble, distribute, evaluate, and organize. The word culture itself, in its specific use, is scarcely older than Kant and its beloved adversary, civilization, did not establish itself—at least in Germany—until the nineteenth century; it was then elevated to the level of a slogan by Spengler. In any case, the present-day proximity of the concepts "culture" and "administration" is easily detected within the practices of language, which in radio broadcasting attach the title "The Cultural Word" to a province where everything possible is encountered, insofar as it corresponds to a more or less precise idea of niveau and cultivation—in contrast to the sphere of entertainment—that province of administration, in other words, which is reserved for a spirit which is not spirit at all, but rather a service to listeners, devoted to light music along with its literary and dramatic pedants.

At the same time, however—according to German concepts—culture is opposed to administration. Culture would like to be higher and more pure, something untouchable which cannot be tailored according to any tactical or technical considerations. In educated language, this line of thought makes reference to the autonomy of culture. Popular opinion even takes pleasure in associating the concept of personality with it. Culture is viewed as the manifestation of pure humanity without regard for its functional relationship within society. In spite of its self-righteous assonance, the word culture cannot be avoided; this proves to what a degree the category, correctly criticized hundreds of times, is both fitting for and dedicated to the world as it is—namely, to the administrated world. Nonetheless, no half-way sensitive person can overcome the discomfort conditioned by his consciousness of a culture which is indeed administrated. As Eduard Steuermann once formulated it, the more that is done for culture, the worse it fares.[2] This paradox could be developed as follows: culture suffers damage when it is planned and administrated; when it is left to itself, however, everything cultural threatens not only to lose its possibility of effect, but its very existence as well. It is neither possible to accept uncritically the concept of culture, long permeated by ideas of departmentalization, nor to continue to shake one's head conservatively about what is being done to culture in the age of integral organization.

The aversion towards the words culture and administration—an aversion by no means free of barbarism and overshadowed by the urge to release the safety catch on a revolver—must not conceal that a certain truth is involved in it. This makes possible the treatment of culture as something of a unity, as for example the heads of cultural departments of cities are wont to do when they unite in the hands of an expert a series of objects which for the moment actually do have something in common. This common factor stands in contrast to everything which serves the reproduction of material life, the literal self-preservation of the human being in general, and the needs of his mere existence. Everyone knows that these boundaries cannot be clearly fixed. From the beginning it has been argued whether the spheres of justice and politics are to be included in culture; they are, at any rate, not to be found in the cultural departments organized by administration. It is further difficult to deny that due to the total tendencies at work in the present, many facets traditionally alloted to culture come to resemble material production more and more: the natural sciences far into the highest reaches of theoretical discipline— "philosophic" according to older ways of thinking, in a manner hardly expected from the traditional perspective of culture—determine to an ever-greater degree the down-to-earth fate of man. The progress of these sciences is, in turn, directly dependent upon the forces of material life, i.e., of economics. This is the situation before which man stands today and which is so discomforting to him. The point is missed, however, if this situation is merely discussed to death by concentrating upon supposedly transitional phenomena. The current inclination to deny embarrassing contradictions in this matter by means of conceptual distinctions and manipulations—a type of vulgarized epistemology—must be resisted. For the moment the simple fact must be recognized that that which is specifically cultural is that which is removed from the naked necessity of life.

This, however, does not offer dispensation from the consideration of the meaning of administration, for this is no longer merely a national or communal institution existing in clear separation from the free play of social forces. The tendency of every institution towards expansion—both quantitatively and qualitatively—was designated as immanent by Max Weber in *The Theory of Social and Economic Organization* (Part III, Chapter VI).[3] Weber did this in keeping with the formally definitional method of his late work. In Weber's view, bureaucracies, following their own law, are destined to expand. In the recent past the Nazi SS offers the most horrid example in support of this thesis. Weber finds the foundation of his thesis in the technical superiority of the organizational type of administration in contrast to traditionalist organization: "The decisive reason for the advance of bureaucratic organization has always been its purely technical superiority over every other form of organization. A fully-developed bureaucratic mechanism stands in the same relationship to other forms as does the machine to the non-mechanical types of production of goods. Precision, speed, clarity, documentary ability, continuity, discretion, unity, rigid subordination, reduction of friction and of material and personal expenses are unique to bureaucratic organization. In the case of monocratic administration, these factors are intensified to the optimum through schooled individual officials in contrast to colleague-like older forms which are either honorary or extra-official" (Weber, 600f). It is precisely the example of the SS, however, which shows to what degree the formal concept of rationality, imputed by Weber and restricted to an end-means relationship, impedes judgment on the rationality of means. In Weber's own theory of rationality, there is a suspicion of the imprint of administrated thought. The mechanism through which independence is established by organizations would have to be defined more specifically than was done by Weber or even in the formal sociology of Simmel, who simply contrasted phenomena of social ossification which life as a metaphysical actuality. Organizations of convenience in an antagonistic society must necessarily pursue particular ends; they do this at the expense of the interests of other groups. Therefore, obduracy and reification necessarily result. If such organizations continued to occupy a subordinate position within which they were totally open and honest towards their membership and its direct desires, they would be incapable of any action. The more firmly integrated they are, the greater is their prospect for asserting themselves in relation to others. The advantage of totalitarian "monolithic" nations over liberalist nations in power politics which can be internationally observed today is also applicable to the structure of organizations of small format. Their external effectivity is a function of their inner homogeneity, which in turn is dependent upon the so-called totality gaining primacy over individual interests, so that the organization *qua* organization takes the place of such interests. An organization is forced into independence by self-preservation; at the same time this establishment of independence leads to alienation from its purposes and from the people of whom it is composed. Finally—in order to be able to pursue its goals appropriately—it enters into a contradiction with them.

It is difficult to accept the immanent tendency of administration towards expansion and the establishment of independence as a simple form of control as the explanation for the transition from administrative apparatuses in the older sense of the word into those of the administrated world, along with their entry into regions not previously subject to administration. Responsibility for this might lie in the extension of conditions of exchange throughout the entirety of life in the face of increasing monopolization. Thinking in equivalents is in itself a form of production insofar as it produces the commensurability of all objects along with their subsumability under abstract rules. Qualitative differences between spheres as well as those within each individual sphere are reduced and therewith the resistance against administration is lessened. At the same time, growing concentration brings about units of such scope that traditionalist—in any way "irrational" methods—are no longer of any help. Economically, risk increases along with the size of the unit and this calls for planning—at least planning of the type demanded up to now by the type in control, defined by Max Weber as the "monocratic" type. However, the immoderate size even of those institutions not concerned about profit— such as education and radio—furthers the practices of administration through the demand for organizational gradation. These practices are strengthened by technological development; in the case of radio, for example, that which is to be communicated is concentrated to the extreme and disseminated as far as possible. Max Weber was still in a position to restrict his thought essentially to administration in the narrow sense, i.e., to bureaucratic hierarchies. He made note—in agreement with Robert Michels—of analogous tendencies only in political parties and, of course, in the sector of education and instruction as well. Meanwhile, this tendency has left all this far behind and achieved total development; this it has done by no means only in economic monopolies. The increase in the quantity of administrative apparatus has brought about a new quality. Mechanisms conceived according to a liberalistic model are no longer roofed over or interpenetrated by administration; they have rather assumed the upper hand towards spheres of freedom to such a degree that the latter appear only to be tolerated. Precisely this was anticipated in the era of pre-fascism by Karl Mannheim.

Even culture is not taboo to this tendency. Within the economic sector, Weber asks whether the understanding of the administrators for the objective problems which they have to solve is equal to the powers which they wield. This is so because precise factual knowledge in their field is a matter of immediate economic existence: "errors in official statistics bring no direct consequences for the guilty official; errors in the calculation of a capitalistic concern result in losses in the firm, indeed, perhaps even in the loss of its existence" (Weber, 673). However, the question regarding the competence of bureaucracies, formulated by Weber in regard to economics, has in the meantime magnified in scope to the same degree as has administration itself within society. This question becomes critical in the cultural sphere. Weber touches upon what is coming in a parenthetical remark without realizing the significance of his observation, made over forty years ago during the conception of his great work. Within the highly-specialized context of the educational-sociological annotation to this chapter on bureaucracy he mentions that the possession of educational patents increasingly represses talent—or "charisma," for the spiritual cost of educational patents is always slight and does not particularly decrease with mass production (Weber, 676). According to this thought, that irrational mission which is not to be planned progressively withdraws from the spirit itself, while this remains a mission for which the spirit is uniquely suited according to traditional views. In an excourse, Weber underscores this view: "Behind all pronouncements of the present day on the bases of education is to be found at some decisive point that struggle of the 'specialist' type against old 'cultured humanity,' a struggle which penetrated into all the most intimate questions of culture and which is conditioned by the irrevocable expansion of the control of all public and private relations through bureaucraticization and the steadily-increasing significance of specialized knowledge" (Weber, 677). Weber's opposition to "specialized humanity" expressed here is of the type common in late-liberal society since Ibsen's *Hedda Gabler*. Inseparable from this, however, is the obligatory increase of administrative control in regions in which administration is without objective competence. Specialists must exercise authority in fields in which they cannot be professionally qualified, while their particular aptitude in abstractly-technical matters of administration is needed in order that the organization continues to function.

The dialectic of culture and administration nowhere expressed the sacrosanct irrationality of culture so clearly as in the continually growing alienation of administration from culture—both in terms of its objective categories and its personal composition. (And culture, of course, seems most thoroughly irrational to those who have had the smallest experience of it). For that which is administrated, administration is an external affair by which it is subsumed rather than comprehended. This is precisely the essence of administrated rationality itself, which does nothing but order and cover over. In the chapter on amphiboly in the *Critique of Pure Reason*, Kant—in opposition to Leibnitz—denied rationality the ability of cognition of the "interior things." Aporia prevails between the absolute purpose of the cultural and the absolute rationality of administration, which is nothing but the rationality of scientific ratio. What is called cultural with good reason must recollectively assimilate whatever has been left along the way in the process of the progressive control of nature, reflected in increasing rationality and ever more rational forms of control. Culture is the perennial claim of the particular over the general, as long as the latter remains unreconciled to the former. At least, this was envisioned in the distinction between the nomothetic and the idiographic—problematic as this distinction might be—made in the Southwest German School towards which Max Weber was philosophically inclined. However, administration necessarily represents—without subjective guilt and without individual will—the general against this particular. The twisted feeling of irreconcilability in the relation of culture and administration is characteristic of this situation. It bears witness to the continuing antagonistic character of a world which is growing ever more unified. The demand made by administration upon culture is essentially heteronomous: culture—no matter what form it takes—is to be measured by norms not inherent to it and which have nothing to do with the quality of the object, but rather with some type of abstract standards imposed from without, while at the same time the administrative instance—according to its own prescriptions and nature—must for the most part refuse to become involved in questions of immanent quality which regard the truth of the thing itself or its objective bases in general. Such expansion of administrative competence into a region, the idea of which contradicts every kind of average generality inherent to the concept of administrative norms, is itself irrational, alien to the immanent ratio of the object—e.g., to the quality of a work of art— and a matter of coincidence as far as culture is concerned. The self-consciousness of this antinomy and the consequences thereof are the first demands which would have to be made upon an administrative praxis which is mature and enlightened in the Kantian sense.

At an early point—beginning around the middle of the nineteenth century—culture began to resist this rationality of purpose. During the age of Symbolism and Art Nouveau, artists such as Oscar Wilde provocatively called culture useless. In bourgeois society, however, a terribly complex relation prevails between the useful and the useless, a situation which is by no means new today. The usefulness of the useful is itself by no means beyond doubt and the useless occupies the place of that which can no longer be distorted by profit. Much which is classified as useful goods goes beyond the directly biological reproduction of life. This reproduction itself is in no sense a great beyond of history, but rather is dependent upon that which is looked upon as culture. If human beings of the industrial era were to spend the days of their existence under those conditions which characterized the vegetative life of the Stone Age, they would no doubt perish. Critical Theory, in its view of society, has expressed this in the hypothesis that reproduction of the labor force corresponds to the cultural state historically achieved by any given age; this is not necessarily a static natural category. It is not necessary to be a follower of the American economist Veblen, back to whom technocracy dates and who tendentiously viewed all goods not drastically necessary as the expression of control, status, and ostentation; he further designated all of culture as that looked upon in the slovenly jargon of the administrated world as "show." It is not possible, however, to be blind to the fact that the useful—that which is of advantage to man in all previous history—is nothing immediate, existing for its own sake, but rather that within the total system which has its eye directed towards profit. The useful *per se* has been relegated to a secondary position, where it is produced by the machinery of the system as well. There is hardly another point to which the consciousness of society is so allergic as it is to this one. Precisely because the usefulness of the useful is so dubious a matter, it is doubly important that this apparatus demonstrate its usefulness through its function solely for the sake of the consumer. For this reason the line of demarcation between the useful and the useless is drawn so strictly in ideology. The enthronement of culture as an entity unto itself, independent of all material conditions—indeed, as something which makes these conditions matters of total indifference—is a fitting correlation of the faith in the pure usefulness of the useful. Culture is looked upon as thoroughly useless and for that reason as something beyond the planning and administrative methods of material production; this results in a much sharper definition of the profile upon which the claim to validity of both the useful and the useless is based. One factor of actuality has manifested itself within this ideology: the separation of culture from the material process of life and—finally—the social hiatus between physical and intellectual work. The heritage of this situation is to be observed in the antinomy of culture and administration. The scent of philistinism which clings to administration is of the same type—and not only philologically—as the odium attached to low, useful, and—in the final analysis—physical labor by antiquity. The rigid opposition of culture and administration in thought, the product of a social and spiritual situation which attempts at the same time to force the two together, has nonetheless always been a questionable matter. In art history it is well known that wherever the artifacts of the past manifest the demand for collective labor—and this extends deep into the individual production of significant architects, sculptors, and painters—administration spoke with a decisive voice. For that reason, even in the past, administration by no means lived in happy harmony with those who today unhesitatingly call themselves the creators of culture—a romantic desire fondly projected backward into history. The church and later the regents of the Italian city states, followed by the princes of absolutism, represented administrative instances from the perspective of their relation to the sphere of culture. Their relation to cultural production was probably far more substantial than that between present-day administration and administrated culture. The undisputed dominance of religion reduced the contrast between culture and practical life; the powerful lords of that day—often enough, to be sure, condottieri—were probably closer to culture than many of the administrative specialists of a society marked by the radical division of labor. This, however, made their control of culture all the more immediate and rigorous, for it was unchecked by any regulations or rational rules of procedure. The relation of the immanent truth of cultural configurations to that which has today been given the dubious name of "commission" was at that time, at any rate, hardly less odious than today. Great artists even of a type which seems by and large to have agreed with the objectively valid spirit of their time—such as Bach—lived in permanent conflict with their administrations. Less is known about such conflicts during the high Middle Ages only because at that time they were pre-decided in favor of the administrative power simply as a matter of principle. In relation to this power, demands which have achieved full consciousness of themselves only in the modern concept of individualism scarcely had a chance.

Despite all this there has been an essential change in the relation between culture and organized power. Culture—as that which goes beyond the system of self-preservation of the species—involves an irrevocably critical impulse towards the status quo and all institutions thereof. This is by no means merely a tendency embodied in many cultural structures, but rather a protest against integration which always violently opposes that which is qualitatively different; in a certain sense this criticism is directly against the idea of leveling unification itself. The fact that anything at all thrives which is different and which is not to be turned into cash illuminates the prevailing praxis in all its dubiousness. It is not only through its manifest practical intentions, but rather through its mere existence— indeed, precisely through its impractical nature—that art manifests a polemic, secretly practical character. This, however, cannot be reconciled through the insertion of culture as a category—"cultural activities"—into the totality of prevailing practice as has been done under current conditions with total smoothness. At one time the line of demarcation between reality and culture was neither so sharp nor so deep as it now is. Works of art did not, for example, reflect upon their own autonomy and upon the formal law unique to each of them; rather they had their place within given contexts, within which they fulfilled a function, no matter how immediate it was. They did not yet assert their existence as works of art to the degree which was later to seem almost a matter of course; it was precisely this factor from which the fullness and comprehensiveness of their success— indeed their very artistic power—benefited. Paul Valéry enlarged upon this topic without falling victim to the balsam-like cliché regarding the human being for whom all things supposedly exist; the human being has become fashionable only since he became fungible. If one reads Vasari's biographies of the painters, one is astonished to note the stress which he placed upon the ability of the painters of the Renaissance to imitate nature—i.e., to create portraits of great similarity to their models—as something particularly worthy of praise. Since the invention of photography, this ability—not easily separated from practical purposes in painting— has become a matter of increasing indifference—an attitude which extends to older painting as well. But even Valéry suspected that such painting owed its aesthetic authenticity to the fact that it had not yet taken an oath to a chemically pure concept of the aesthetic, implying that, in the final analysis, art might exist as art only where it no longer expressed any ambition as art. This attitude involved the full awareness on the part of art that its previous innocence was not to be reestablished through an imagined communal will.

At any rate, the concept of culture has been neutralized to a great extent through its emancipation from the actual processes of life experienced with the rise of bourgeoisie and the Enlightenment. The opposition of culture to the status quo has been deadened to a large degree. Hegel's late and resigned theory which reserves the concept of absolute spirit—in contrast to his views in the *Phenomenology*—only for cultural spheres in the narrower sense is the first and up until now is still the most significant theoretical imprint of this state of affairs. The process of neutralization—the transformation of culture into something independent and external, removed from any possible relation to praxis—makes it possible to integrate it into the organization from which it untiringly cleanses itself; furthermore, this is accomplished neither with contradiction nor with danger. Today manifestations of extreme artistry can be fostered, produced and presented by official institutions; indeed, art is dependent upon such support if it is to be produced at all and to find its way to an audience. Yet, at the same time, art denounces everything institutional and official. This gives some evidence of the neutralization of culture and of the irreconcilability with administration of that which has been neutralized. Through the sacrifice of its possible relation to praxis, the cultural concept itself becomes an instance of organization; that which is so provokingly useless in culture is transformed into tolerated negativity or even into something negatively useful—into a lubricant for the system, into something which exists for something else, into untruth, or into goods of the culture industry calculated for the consumer. All this is registered today in the uncomfortable relation between culture and administration.

Nothing escapes the attention of radically socialized society,[4] which further affects the culture of which it seizes control. This can be illustrated in simple fashion. Sometime ago a small publication—a pamphlet—appeared apparently written for the needs of those who undertake cultural trips through Europe—of whatever use such a brochure might possibly be. It offered a concise catalogue of artistic festivals during this particular summer and the autumn as well. The reason for such a scheme is obvious: it permits the cultural traveler to divide his time and to seek out that which he thinks will be of interest to him—in short, he can plan his trip according to the same principle which lies behind the organization of these festivals: they are all embraced and controlled by a single comprehensive organization. Inherent in the idea of the festival, however—and of the the artistic festival as well, no matter how secularized and weakened it might be—is the claim to something unique, to the emphatic event which is not fungible. Festivals are to be celebrated as they come; they are not to be organized only from the perspective of avoiding overlapping. Administrative reason which takes control of them and rationalizes them banishes festivity from them. This results in an intensification into the grotesque which cannot escape the notice of the more sensitive nerves present at these so-called cultural offerings—even at those of the avant garde. In an effort to preserve a feeling of contrast to contemporary streamlining, culture is still permitted to drive about in a type of gypsy wagon; the gypsy wagons, however, roll about secretly in a monstrous hall, a fact which they themselves do not notice.

This might well explain to no small degree the loss of inner tension which is to be observed today at various points even in progressive cultural productions—to say nothing of the less progressive efforts. Whatever raises from within itself a claim to being autonomous, critical and antithetical—while at the same time never being able to assert this claim with total legitimacy—must necessarily come to naught; this is particularly true when its impulses are integrated into something heteronomous to them, which has been worked out previously from above—that is to say, when it is granted the space in which to draw breath immediately by that power against which it rebels. At the same time, this is not a result of the easily-criticized excesses of managerism gone wild. In the administrated world managers are used as scapegoats almost as frequently as are the bureaucrats; the assignment of objective guilt relationships to people is itself a product of prevailing ideology. Paradox developments are unavoidable. The total social and economic tendency consumes the material basis of traditional culture, either liberal or individualistic in style. The appeal to the creators of culture to withdraw from the process of administration and keep distant from it has a hollow ring. Not only would this deprive them of the possibility of earning a living, but also of every effect, every contact between work of art and society, something which the work of greatest integrity cannot do without, if it is not to perish. Those who praise the purity of their withdrawal from organization—those quiet voices in the nation—arouse the suspicion that they are provincial and petit bourgeois reactionaries. The popular argument that the material basis for the productive spirit—and this always has meant the non-conforming spirit—has always been precarious and that this spirit has preserved its power in defiant self-assertion is threadbare. The fact that an undesirable condition is nothing which has set in just today is no reason for perpetuating it if this condition is no longer necessary; that better things will make their way by virtue of their own power is nothing but an edifying ginger-bread slogan. "Much is lost in the night." From time to time coincidental discoveries—such as that of Georg Büchner by Karl Emil Franzos—give an idea of the senseless destruction which has taken place in the history of mankind, even in the sphere of spiritual production. Furthermore, there has been a qualitative change in this region. There no longer are any hiding places—not even in Europe which in this respect, as in so many others, involuntarily imitates America; there is no longer dignity in poverty—not even any longer the possibility of modesty surviving the winter for a person who loses his position in the administrated world. It is sufficient to call to mind an existence such as that of Paul Verlaine at the end of the nineteenth century: the lift of the fallen alcoholic who, even when he was down and out, found friendly and understanding doctors in Paris hospitals who supported him in the midst of the most extreme of extreme situations. Anything similar would be unthinkable today. Not that there is any lack of such doctors or of friendly people in general—in a certain sense the administrated would has witnessed in many areas an increase in humanitarianism from the perspective of concern on the part of everyone for everyone. It is just that such doctors—with an eye towards their administrations—would probably no longer have the right to give shelter to the vagabond genius, to honor him and to protect him from humiliation. Instead, he would become the object of public welfare, attended and fed and treated with great care, to be sure, but torn from his way of life and therewith presumably from the possibility of expressing that which he had once felt to be the purpose of his life in the world—no matter how dubious the attitude towards the production of the definitively degraded and rejected Verlaine was. The concept of socially useful work cannot be separated from the process of integral socialization; it would necessarily also be held up to the person whose usefulness can be defined only in terms of the negation of this process and salvation would hardly turn out to be a blessing to the man saved today.

To become aware of such situations, it is by no means necessary to concentrate upon that customarily defined following the second war by the fatally neutralizing word "border situation"—"Grenz-situation"—although it is clear that such situations—extreme situations—are in themselves inseparable from the substantiality of everything cultural down to the present day: in this region the concept of "the average" has no place. The changes in the basic social stratum of culture, which is the matter of central concern here, extend into more harmless regions. In Vienna of the 1920's within the Schoenberg circle the strength of tradition among the anti-traditionalists—both in terms of art and of general personal conduct—was surprising. The spirit which attracted people to this circle was decidedly artistic, selective, and sensitive; it bore within itself the markings of discriminatory competence and a sense of history. These artists—prepared for the dissolution of established ideas and norms— existed with a certain naivete and matter-of-factness within Austrian society, which remained half-closed and half-feudal even after the fall of the monarchy. It is precisely to this society that they owe that sensuous culture and impatient subtlety which brought them into conflict with Viennese conformism. The boldness of artistic renewal joined hands with proud negligence. In spite of all irony and skepticism, numerous categories of a still firmly integrated social and spiritual order were accepted. These categories provided a not inconsiderable prerequisite for the insubordinate tenderness of this generation. It was necessary, as it were, to be satiated with tradition in order really to be able to negate it and to be able to turn the unique vital force of tradition against ossification and self-satisfaction. It is only where that which was is still strong enough to form the forces within the subject and at the same time to oppose them that the production of that which has not yet been seems possible. Constructivism and green houses can be conceived only under conditions of warmth and within psychologically protected dwellings—and this is not to be understood only in literal terms.

However, the equalization of the tensions felt today between culture and its objective conditions threatens culture with spiritual death by freezing. In its relation to reality there is a dialectic of non-simultaneity. Only where the development towards the administered world and social modernity had not yet asserted itself so successfully—in France and Austria, for example—did the aesthetically modern—the avant garde—thrive. When reality, however, dwells upon the current standard, a tendentious levelling of consciousness takes place. The more easily consciousness adjusts to integral reality, the more it is discouraged from going beyond that which is there once and for all.

Naturally, by no means all cultural spheres are subject to this dialectic of non-simultaneity; many of them are actually in need of the newest administrative standards. This is true of the whole community of natural sciences which probably both absorb and also produce the strongest productive forces today. They could not do justice to their present-day assignments in any other way than through the aid in planning offered by administration; the rationality of sciences is itself similar to that of administration. The same situation exists wherever team work, collective effort, and wide-range investigation are necessary, such as in empirical social research. This field has not only modeled its own training after the example of administrative categories; without administration, it would sink into chaos—above all, into that which is coincidentally particular and irresponsible. Even art could not possibly oppose all this en bloc. A field such as architecture, which—by virtue of its foundation in practical needs—is today better off than the autonomous artistic genres, was never conceivable without administration. The film, above all, because of the scope of costs which can be met only through investment, is dependent upon a type of planning analogous to that of public administration. In the film, to be sure, the contradiction between inescapably calculating and the truth of matters is defined with horrifying clarity: the foolishness of the film is not so much the product of individual failure as of this contradiction. Its principle is the planning intention which includes the cinema-goer in its calculation; this results in the lack of harmony.

Administration, however, is not simply imposed upon the supposedly productive human being from without. It multiplies within this person himself. That a particular situation in time brings forth those subjects intended for it is to be taken very literally. Nor are those who produce culture secure before the "increasingly organic composition of mankind" (cf. Adorno, *Minima Moralia*, 442).[5] Their security terminates in the situation in which their own participation in the administrative apparatus spreads out before them in opposition to spontaneity in much the same way in which it manifests itself within material production. Whoever possesses a flair for such tendencies can expect to encounter disguised administrative categories even in the most advanced avant garde artistic products—indeed, even in the most finely-nuanced emotions of the individual, in his voice and gestures. Attention must be directed toward aesthetic tendencies in the direction of integral construction; this can be verified at many junctures. Such tendencies envision a type of planning from above, the analogy of which to administration is not to be ignored. Such structures might well be totally predetermined. According to Max Weber's thesis, administration, by its very nature, by and large excludes individual arbitrariness in favor of an objectively regulated process; in the same manner the individual action of the idea in art of this type is frowned upon. At the same time, the applied methods of procedures are not arbitrarily thought out—and this is what gives the phenomenon its weight—but rather developed with an immanently artistic consequence. These methods can be traced back very far into history (cf. Adorno, *Klangfiguren*, 95).[6] But it is precisely art which gives total voice to the seemingly individual and coincidental which is now to be the subject of total aesthetic prohibition and which in turn must pay the price for progressive integration presenting a totally different situation than that found in actual administration. Within certain boundaries, administration— through rational ordering processes—actually prevents negative coincidence, blind control over others, nepotism, and favoritism. Ever since Aristotle's *Politics*, it has been well-known that the shadow of injustice falls upon the just rational law within the order of reality so that the rationality of administrative acts stands in need of that corrective which Aristotle included as "equity." The work of art is limited by this residue to the same degree. To the work of art clings an impulse of that which is ordered and produced from without—secretly of that subjectivism which is indeed anathema. Today the field of tension within all advanced art is actually defined by the poles of radical construction and equally radical resistance against it; often both factors merge. Furthermore, it is from this perspective that tachism is to be understood.[7] The negation of the concept of the cultural is itself under preparation. The major factor therein is the dismissal of such concepts as autonomy, spontaneity, and criticism: autonomy, because the subject, rather than making conscious decisions, both has and wishes to subjugate itself to whatever has been preordained. The reason for this is that the spirit, which according to traditional cultural concepts should be its own law-giver, at every instant now experiences its own impotence in relation to the overwhelming demands of mere being. Spontaneity diminishes because total planning takes precedence over the individual impulse, predetermining this impulse in turn, reducing it to the level of illusion, and no longer tolerating that play of forces which was expected to give rise to a free totality. And finally, criticism is dying out because the critical spirit is as disturbing as sand in a machine to that smoothly-running operation which is becoming more and more the model of the cultural. This critical spirit now seems antiquated, irresponsible, and unworthy, much like "arm chair" thinking. The relationship between generations has been reversed ludicrously; youth seeks its validation in the principle of reality while the older generation digresses into the intelligible world. The National Socialists, who anticipated all this in brutal fashion—thereby unmasking it paradistically—were in relation to the category of the critical precisely the heralds of a coming development; this was manifested in their replacement of criticism with their own observations upon art, which in actuality offered only information on factual matters. This same tendency is to be noted in the increasing suppression of the critical spirit today; a journal of the avant garde proudly displays the sub-title "Information."

In many sectors the accounts have not yet been balanced; this is particularly true of those regions isolated or distant from the most powerful social tendencies, although they hardly benefit from their isolation. In official culture, on the other hand, the accounts balance all the more perfectly. UNESCO poets actually come into being who are, for example, capable of enthusiasm because the humane blossoms in the midst of inhuman situations; in the name of a humanitarianism which steers clear of any controversial issue, they inscribe the international slogans of high administration with their very hearts' blood. Nothing need be said about the infantile trash to which the authorities of government and party obligate artists. No one would be astonished if in the West projects were financed involving research on generally valid, absolute values, conducted, however, with the under-developed countries in the back of the mind. There is no lack of obliging intellectuals ready to cast suspicions upon the critical spirit of true intellectuals through an affirmation of life borrowed from want-ad marriage offers. This official picture of humanism is completed by accusing everything truly human and in no way official of inhumanity. For criticism takes from man his meagre spiritual possessions, removing the veil which he himself looks upon as benevolent. The anger aroused in him by the unveiled image is diverted to those who tear this veil, in keeping with the hypothesis of Helvetius that truth never damages anyone except him who utters it. My by no means new observation (cf. *Minima Moralia*, 395ff)[8] that even that which deviates is by no means secure from standardization has recently been misused to discredit the polemic application of the concept of conformism—as if the fact that there is a second-rate conformism, preceded at least by an act of resistance, somehow makes more palatable the first spineless conformism, that swimming along with the current and simultaneous adjustment to stronger batallions. In truth—to borrow a word from Heinrich Regius—one attacks the word conformism, because one is in total agreement with the process defined by it.[9]

A further particularly clear phenomenon to which the label of the Muses is attached has its place in administrated culture; this is the attempt —effective in terms of mass psychology—to save the spontaneity which is threatened by administration or—as they refer to it in those circles— through "correct understanding": every attempt of pedagogy to lay claim to the spiritual is an expression of this desire. The visible result is regression, blind complacency on the part of the subject encouraged to be spontaneous. It is no accident that the jargon of authenticity is spoken everywhere in these spheres, the language of which Karl Korn has offered such penetrant examples in his recent books on language in the administrated world.[10] Particularly understanding in this regard is the chapter on pretense. This jargon is not identical with the administrative language of older vintage, as it can be encountered still today in old filing cabinets haunted by the tone of its touchingly subaltern notes. The old administrative language—dust-covered and antiquated—bears significant witness to the relative separation of administration and culture, whereby—against its will—it pays homage to culture. The jargon of authenticity, however, united the heterogeneous under one roof. Linguistic components from an individual sphere—from theological tradition, existential philosophy, the youth movement, the military of from Expressionism—are institutionally absorbed and then—to a certain extent—returned to the private sphere, placed back in the possession of the individual person, who can then speak with ease, freedom, and joy about mission and encounter, about authentic pronouncement and concern, as though he himself were pleased. In truth, he is only putting on airs, as though each individual were his own announcer on FM radio. If, for example, a letter contains the phrase "in approximately," the reader can assume that a few lines later the writer of the letter will announce his attention of approaching the person addressed in the near future. The personal contact stipulated in this way is nothing but the mask of an administrative process which draws the person thus addressed into its function: humanity which can be turned on and off should inspire the person addressed to unpaid achievements.

Nonetheless, what is demonstrated by such models is to be attributed to administration, in regard to which one might console oneself by means of a philosophically disreputable concept of inwardness or with pure culture

which is guaranteed genuine. Those who use such words are the first
to attack everything unregimented in a rage. In truth, culture itself is
expected to pay the bill. Even when culture is viewed as something removed
from reality, it is in no way isolated from reality, but rather involves
instructions for actual realization, no matter how distant and mediated
this might be. If culture is totally deprived of this impulse, it becomes
invalid. Within culture, administration only repeats the offenses committed
by culture itself in that it ever degraded itself to an element of representation, to a field of activity, and, finally, to a sector of mass action,
of propaganda and of tourism. If culture is defined as the de-barbarization
of man, elevating him beyond the state of simple nature, without actually
perpetuating this state through violent suppression, then culture is a total
failure. It has not been able to take root in man as long as he has lacked
the prerequisites for an existence marked by human dignity. It is no
coincidence that he is still capable of barbarous outbursts because of
suppressed rancor about his fate, about his deeply-felt lack of freedom.
The fact that he welcomes the trash of the culture industry with outstretched
arms—half aware that it is trash—is another aspect of the same state of
affairs, the seeming harmlessness of which is probably restricted to the
surface. Culture long ago evolved into its own contradiction, the congealed
content of educational privilege; for that reason it now takes its place
within the material production process as an administrated supplement
to it.

Furthermore, whoever resists being convinced that it is necessary
to bring on something ominously positive immediately is not going to be
content to step aside shaking his head once he has taken stock of all
these difficulties, simply because the objective possibility of anything better
is blocked. The radicalism which promises itself everything by virtue of
total change is abstract; for even within the changed totality the problems
of the individual obstinately return again. Such radicalism loses ground
as soon as its idea volatilizes into a chimera, dispensing every further
effort toward improvement. Within itself, it then becomes an agent to
sabotage something better. Excessive demand is a sublime form of sabotage. On the other hand, it is not be overlooked that in the question
regarding what is to be done here and now, a type of total social subject
is imagined, a community of *hommes de bonne volonté* who need only
take their places around a gigantic round table in order to bring order

into this chaos of failure. But the difficulties of the cultural, for which the commonplace concept of crisis is no longer in any way sufficient, are so deeply rooted that individual good will is severely restricted. There is no point in imagining a unanimous will where objective and subjective antagonism provokes disaster. Finally, the threat experienced by the spirit in the fact of rationalization is an indication that the irrationality of the entire situation continues unchanged and that every particular rationalization benefits this irrationality in that it strengthens the pressures of a blind and unreconciled generality upon the particular.

The antinomy of planning and culture results in the dialectical idea of absorbing that which is still spontaneous and not planned into planning, of creative space for these factors and of a strengthening of their possibilities. This idea does not dispense with the basis of social justice. The possibility of decentralization, particularly in view of the state of the forces of technical production as they now approach Utopian dimensions, is favorable to it. Planning of the non-planned within a specific sector—that of education—was emphatically advocated by Helmut Becker; there are other fields which offer analogous situations.[11]

In spite of this seeming plausibility, however, the feeling of untruth cannot be overcome totally: namely, the feeling that the non-planned is degraded to a costume of itself and, consequently, that the freedom involved becomes a fiction. One need only compare the synthetic artists' quarter of New York, Greenwich Village, with the Parisian *rive gauche* of pre-Hitler days. In the New York district license continues to exist as an officially tolerated institution; for this reason it has become what the Americans call "phony." Furthermore, in the tendency to reserve for artists a particular life style—a tendency which dominated the entire nineteenth century—and to permit them to give form to that which is repulsive to the bourgeois society from which they live has concealed the deception exploited perhaps for the first time by Murger's bohème novel.[12]

Planning of the non-planned would have to establish at the outset the degree to which it is compatible with the specific content of the non-planned, i.e., to what degree planning from this perspective is "rational." Beyond this lies the question regarding the impersonal "one"—the person, that is, who represents the instance which makes decisions on the greatest difficulties. In the beginning nothing more can be demanded than a cultural policy, thought out within itself and aware of these difficulties—a policy which does not conceive of the concept of culture as a reified fixed configuration of values, but rather a policy which absorbs critical considerations in order to develop them further. Such a cultural policy would not misunderstand itself as god-willed; it would not blindly endorse faith in culture, blind to its entanglement with the social totality—and for that very reason truly entangled—it would find a parallel in the negative naiveté involved in accepting administration as faith: i.e., whoever receives an office from god, receives ratio from him as well. Administration which wishes to do its part must renounce itself; it needs the ignominious figure of the expert. No city administration, for example, can decide from which painter it should buy paintings, unless it can rely upon people who have a serious, objective and progressive understanding of painting. In establishing the necessity of the expert, one immediately exposes himself again to every imaginable reproach—to the notorious accusation, for example, that the judgement of an expert remains a judgement for experts and as such ignores the community from which—according to popular phraseology—public institutions receive their mandate, or that the expert —necessarily an administrator himself—makes his decision from on high, thus extinguishing spontaneity; furthermore, his authority is not always secure and, among other things, it is a difficult matter to distinguish him from the apparatchik. Although one might be willing to concede the correctness of some of the aspects mentioned here, distrust toward the argument of the man on the street that culture does after all have something to contribute to the life of man will remain: the state of consciousness according to which one is to orient himself from the perspective of this argumentation is in truth the very state of consciousness which would have to be overcome by any culture sufficient to its own concept. All too much pleasure is found in attacks upon exposed modern art, coupled with attacks against administrations which supposedly wasted the pennies of the taxpayer on experiments which the latter viewed either with indifference or rejection. This argumentation is of an illusory democracy; an off-shoot of that totalitarian technique tries to gain life through the exploitation of plebicite forms of democracy. What such voices of the popular soul hate most is anything of free spirit; they sympathize with stale reaction. While the total social constitution formally guarantees equal rights, it nontheless continues to conserve the educational privilege, granting the possibility of differentiated and progressive spiritual experience to only a few. The platitude of the progress of spiritual things—particularly of art—proceeds in the beginning against the will of the majority, makes it possible for the mortal enemies of all progress to entrench themselves behind those who—without any guilt of their own, to be sure—are excluded from the vital expression of their own concern. A cultural policy which has rid itself of social naiveté must see through this complex without fear of the mass of majorities. Through cultural policy alone it is hardly possible to eradicate the contradiction between democratic order and the actual consciousness of those who are kept in a continuing state of minority by social conditions. But democracy through representation, to which even the experts in the administration of cultural matters owe their legitimation, nonetheless permits a certain balance; it makes possible the hindrance of maneuvers which serve barbarism through the corruption of the idea of objective quality by means of callous appeal to the common will. Walter Benjamin's thought on critics whose task it is to uphold the interest of the public against the public itself can be applied to cultural policy as well. To serve this purpose is the duty of the expert. The longing for individuals who might work beyond the realm of expertise usually characterizes only regression or the desire for technicians of communication, with whom—simply because they are lacking any real understanding of matters—one can get along better and who dwell all the more conformingly within their own policy. There is no pure immediacy of culture: wherever it permits itself to be consumed arbitrarily by a public as consumer goods, it manipulates people. The subject becomes the subject of culture only through the mediation of objective discipline; the advocate thereof—in the administrated world, at any rate—is the expert. To be sure, it might be possible to find experts whose authority really is founded upon the authority of the thing itself, rather than in the power of suggestion or personal prestige. It would take an expert to decide who the experts are—and this leads into a vicious circle. The relation between administration and expert is not only a matter of necessity, but it is a virtue as well. It opens a perspective for the protection of cultural matters from the realm of control by the market, which today unhesitatingly mutilates culture. The spirit in its autonomous form is no less alienated from the manipulated and by now firmly-fixed needs of consumers than it is from administration. The authoritarian establishment of the independence of the latter allows

it—through the cooptation of those to whom these matters are not alien—
to make certain corrections in the dictates of these needs. This would
scarcely be possible if the sphere of culture were left totally at the mercy
of the mechanics of supply and demand—to say nothing of the power
of direct command by totalitarian rulers. The most questionable aspect
of the administrated world—this very independence of the executive
instances—conceals the potential of something better; the institutions are
strengthened to such a degree that they—even if they and their function
is transparent to themselves—are able to break through the principle of
merely existing for something else—of adjustment to the deceptive wishes
of a plebicite. These wishes, were they to be fulfilled, would irrevocably
repress everything cultural by bringing it forth from its presumed state
of isolation. If the administrated world is to be understood as one from
which all hiding places are fast disappearing, it should still be possible
for this world to compensate for this and—by virtue of the powers of
men of insight—to create centers of freedom as they are eradicated by
the blind and unconscious process of mere social selection. That irrationality expressed in the independence of administration in its relation
to society is the refuge of the inhibited development of culture itself. It
is only through deviation from prevalent rationality that culture displays
its ratio. Such hopes, however, are rooted in a state of consciousness
on the part of administrators which is by no means simply to be taken
for granted: it would depend upon their critical independence from the
power and the spirit of a consumer society identical with the administrated
world itself.

All the suggestions heard thus far would amount to ideas with broken
wings, were it not for a bit of false logic encountered in them. One adjusts
all too readily to the prevailing conviction that the categories of culture
and administration must simply be accepted as that into which they actually
have developed to a large degree in historical terms: as static blocks which
discretely oppose each other—as mere actualities. In so doing one remains
under the spell of that reification, the criticism of which is inherent in
all the more cogent reflections upon culture and administration. No matter
how reified both categories are in reality, neither is totally reified; both
refer back to living subjects—just as does the most adventurous cybernetic
machine. Therefore, the spontaneous consciousness, not yet totally in
the grips of reification, is still in a position to alter the function of the

institution within which this consciousness expresses itself. For the present, within liberal-democratic order, the individual still has sufficient freedom within the institution and with its help to make a modest contribution to its correction. Whoever makes critically and unflinchingly conscious use of the means of administration and its institutions is still in a position to realize something which would be different from merely administrated culture. The minimal differences from the ever-constant which are open to him define for him—no matter how hopelessly—the difference concerning the totality; it is, however, in the difference itself—in divergence—that hope is concentrated.

Notes

1. "Kultur und Verwaltung" was first delivered as a lecture and then published in *Vorträge, gehalten anlässlich der Hessischen Hochschulwochen für staatswissenschaftliche Fortbildung*, Vol. 28 (Bad Homburg, 1960). It appeared in *Merkur*, Vol. 14 No. 2 (February, 1960), pp. 101-121, which is the basis of this translation. It has since been reprinted in *Soziologica* II (1962). This translation is by Wes Blomster who also supplied the notes. Reprinted with permission from *Telos: A Journal of Critical Social Thought*, 37 (Fall, 1978), pp. 93-111.

2. Steuermann (1892-1964) was among the outstanding pianists of the twentieth century and the major pianistic interpretor and spokesman for Arnold Schoenberg and his school. Steuermann came to the United States in 1936; he taught at the Philadelphia Conservatory and at the Juilliard School. Upon Steuermann's death, Adorno wrote his "Nachruf auf einen Pianisten" ("Eulogy for a Pianist"), included in *Impromptus* (Frankfurt, 1968).

3. *Wirtschaft und Gesellschaft* (Tübingen, 1922). The English translation by A. M. Henderson and Talcott Parsons was published in Glencoe, IL, in 1947. Page references here are to the German edition.

4. Original: "die radikal vergesellschaftete Gesellschaft."

5. Adorno quotes from "Novissimum Organum," Section 147 of *Minima Moralia* (Frankfurt, 1951).

6. Reference is made to "Zur Vorgeschichte der Reihenkomposition" ("On the Pre-History of Serial Composition"), in *Klangfiguren* (Berlin and Frankfurt, 1959).

7. Tachism is a technique of painting which emerged after the second world war. The designation is derived from the French word *tache*—spot, blob, stain. Painters employing this technique throw paint upon the canvas in spots or blobs; they emphasize automatism and spontaneity and deny any intention of producing

conscious formal configurations. Jackson Pollock is a major exponent of this technique.

8. Reference is made to "Piperdruck," Section 132 of Adorno's book.

9. Max Horkheimer published under the pseydonym "Heinrich Regius" in the 1930's; this made possible the circulation of his work in Germany following his own exile from the country.

10. *Sprache in der verwalteten Welt*, 2nd. edition (Olten and Freiburg in Breisgau, 1959).

11. Helmut Becker (born 1913) is Director of Educational Research at the Max Planck Society in Berlin and Professor of Sociology at the Berlin Free University; he has been involved extensively in educational projects of the Aspen Institute for Humanistic Studies. He is the son of Carl Heinrich Becker, who in 1921 and from 1925 to 1930 was German Minister for Cultural Affairs.

12. Henri Murger (1822-1861) published *Scénes de la vie de bohème* in 1847; Puccini's popular opera is based on this work.

The Function of

Crisis: The

Theory / Practice

Split in Planning

Helen Liggett

**College of Urban Affairs
Cleveland State Univ.**

1. The Continuing Political Crisis in Planning

> In American city planning we are burdened with an unfortunately deep distinction between the ideas of academic students of planning and the actions of the working planners.
> John Dyckman

THIS STATEMENT IS FROM an address by John W. Dyckman entitled "Three Crises of American Planning: Planning, Professionalism and the University." The other two interrelated crises he alludes to are: "First and foremost . . . American ambivalence about public planning itself" (280) and our "lack" of "the vision of what kind of state and what kind of politics we want" (293).

Dyckman's concerns about the disjuncture between the promise and practice of planning and the politics of the planning profession continue to be major issues in the field (Faludi 1973, Dear and Scott 1981, Paris 1982, Dear 1986). Most recently, Michael Brooks' pessimistic assessment of "the soul of the profession" in the Spring 1988 issue of the *Journal of the American Planning Association* has sparked spirited commentary (Teitz 1989, Weiss 1989, Cisneros 1989, Marcuse 1989). M. Christine Boyer only put it in the bluntest terms when she asked, "why the planning dialogue in pursuit of an order for the American city persisted over decades in spite of its obvious failure to implement its plans" (1983: ix).

This raises the question of what a crisis is. Paul de Man (1983: 8) argues that crisis implies a criticism at the level of the mode of representation rather than at the level of the activity itself. For example, if we evaluate an activity such as art we are working within a set of assumptions about what constitutes art. A piece is judged as more (good art) or less (bad art) in conformity with non-problematic notions of what art is (and ought to be). To say a crisis exists in art implies criticism at the level of questioning what art itself is.

The Brooks exchange, noted above, displays criticism at this level. Michael Brooks represents planning and planning history as a fall from a former state of grace due to "choices" made within the profession. In response, Peter Marcuse contends that the planning profession should not be represented as an actor in the sense implied by the syntax of "choice," but rather that it should be seen as an evolving practice subject to external forces. Michael Teitz argues that both approaches are reflective of the ideological biases of the authors. Mark Weiss agrees and offers an alternative account of planning and suggests that the "facts" show that planning has always been involved in the economic development of cities—some of it good and some of it bad.

This debate operates on the level of representation, or to use Clifford Geertz's famous phase, it is about "stories we tell ourselves about ourselves." Dyckman's assessment that crises existed in planning may have been appropriate to his time; using de Man's notion of crisis it appears that same assessment is relevant today. That the leading journal in the field frequently publishes debates about what planning is and should be indicates how persistent the crisis of representation is when practice is assumed to reflect theory.

The only commentary by a non-academic planner in the Brooks debate is by The Honorable Henry C. Cisneros, Mayor of San Antonio, who writes less about planners and how planners should understand themselves and more about the current situation in urban areas. He treats planners as unproblematic allies and suggests that given the problems facing cities due to economic restructuring and shifting governmental priorities, planners with vision will be needed in the future. Some planning students take a similar tack. In many departments, there has been recurring concern among students that they learn "what planners really do." An implicit and unitary model of the planner as practical/helper/technician guides these complaints. This model fits in nicely with what Cisneros seems to be calling for because both the model and Cisneros assume that planning is about "problem solving" in a way that does not reflect how discursive practices constitute both problems and possibilities for particular solutions. Thus on the one hand, we have the academically based planners in the Brooks debate addressing planning and politics with concerns about adequate representation, and, on the other hand, we have a practitioner and would-be practitioners addressing planning and politics with concern about appropriate action.

This suggests that at least two of Dykeman's figurations of the continuing crisis in planning are still relevant. The "unfortunately deep distinction between the ideas of the academic students of planning and the actions of the working planners" (282), and our "lack" of a "vision of what kind of state and what kind of politics we want" (293) continue to characterize the discipline.

This paper explores the extent to which the perpetuation of the theory/practice split as a customary form of representation within the field contributes to the continuation of Dykeman's (and Brooks, et al.) recognition of our lack of "vision of what kind of state and what kind of politics we want." I argue that the break between planning theory and planning practice has been conditioned by conventional modes of analysis and customary biases in planning. I suggest alternative frames for writing about planning and planning problems as a means of providing more powerful tools for reflection on the function of this common configuration, the debates surrounding it within the discipline and finally the politics of planning practice in the academy and in professional settings.

2. The Applicability of Poststructural Analysis to the Development of Planning Criticism

Speculation in contemporary language philosophy on the implications of the impossibility of unmediated experience has influenced modes of analysis in both the social sciences and in literary criticism. The search for "the truth of the object" has been impugned and attention has turned to the operation of language. Thus a series of different but related modes of analysis are being developed within the framework of this broad epistemological shift from referential theories of languages to active theories of language. Poststructuralism in particular enables the development of a criticism of planning. If planning is seen from within the frame of contemporary language theory, then the search for "the truth of planning" or inquiry into what planning "really is" must be replaced by analysis of the various contexts in which the discourse of planning takes place. The level of inquiry moves from planning to modes of planning discourse.

The structuralist model, borrowing heavily from anthropology and linguistics, emphasizes language as a more or less static system which is "laid over" events, constituting them into meaningful order. According to the conservative structuralism of Lévi-Strauss, dilemmas in the human condition are solved by the invention of systems of coded oppositions appearing in cultural systems. In Roland Barthes' early radical Marxist oriented structuralism, codes operate to mystify more fundamental systems of dominating relations in the social order. Important historical-structural analysis of planning reveal a relationship between the promises of planning theory to rationalize the urban order and the orientation of planning practice towards the enhancement of capitalism (Boyer 1983, Fainstein and Fainstein 1983, and Foglesong 1986). These studies inform the critical project undertaken here; that is, to understand the function of the opposition between theory and practice within the discipline.

A structuralist approach can lead the planning critic to posit a system of rules or a code within which planning appears. This approach reifies the separation between planning theory and planning practice. The analysis would be "already always" set up to illustrate how planning practice fails to live up to planning theory and/or how planning theory fails to be relevant to planning practice. In the example explicated at length later in this essay, the recent interest within planning theory in developing case studies of practice makes practice into an object of appraisal for academic planners. Research into practice can become an investigation of how practitioners behave, using conventional social science methodology (for examples, see Checkoway 1986). This only constitutes planning practice as an object of research, subject to the academic (theoretical) gaze and ignores the wider implications of poststructuralist thought for extending the fields of analysis to objects, subjects, and the relations between them (for an example of an analysis of local planning practice that does use a poststructuralist approach, see Milroy 1988). For planning criticism to be useful to the current crisis in planning as Dykeman and

Boyer describe it, planners must utilize approaches which do not repeat the convention of opposing theory to practice.

In contrast to the structuralists, Pierre Bourdieu (1977) argues that systems of representation are not static codes simply applied "over" events—they work. Practical wisdom or strategies are entailed in the work of maintaining social life. He emphasizes this point when he suggests that as we think of social practices as generative in terms of prevailing theories; we must also think of them involving the exercise of judgment in everyday life situations. In other words, working out what is possible in practical terms is a mode by which theories of practice are generated and maintained. Phrasing it particularly aptly, Bourdieu (1977: 8) argues that to guard against an over structuralist view, analysts need to recognize "the 'art' of the necessary improvisation which defines excellence." In relation to developing a planning criticism, this requires recognizing that planning theory in the academy is a practice and that planning professionals operate within the context of enabling theories.

Using Bourdieu's poststructuralism to analyze the production of meaning makes it possible to move beyond the limitations embodied in the expectation that academic planning should inform (and inform on) planning practice. The discursive politics of planning in the academy and in the field and the relations between the two can become subjects to be analyzed at the constitutive level.

In other words, poststructuralist approaches re-open the question of how language works by challenging, among other things, overly objectivist views of language and emphasizing instead the slippage of meaning among codes and the involvement of different levels of language in the production of meaning. Deconstruction, which has been central to the move from structuralism to poststructuralism illuminates this project. Deconstruction is summarized by Flores in the following way: "1) the noticing of binary oppositions and their hierarchizing or totalizing effects; 2) the inversion and dismantling of the oppositions; 3) the preclusion of the emergence of a synthesizing term that would produce a new hierarchy of totalization" (cited by Corlett 1987).

To begin a poststructuralist analysis of the crisis in planning is to begin a critical examination of the operation of the opposition between theory and practice itself as a taken-for-granted form in representations of planning.

3. The Habit of Maintaining a Distinction
Between Planning Theory and Planning Practice

The current conventions in planning which separate theory from practice conspire against the analysis of the politics of planning at the constitutive level. An implicit hierarchy is enforced between theory and practice which leads to the exclusion of inquiry into the relation between the two. This re-enforces the idea that formulating a true or right way to plan is an important goal of the profession. The search for the "real" planning has produced theories of planning which decontextualize it completely: such as in the case of theories of procedural planning, theories of planning which contextualize planning practice in terms of a predetermined meta-narrative as in a neo-Marxist analysis, and theories which separate these two approaches from each other. Such maneuvers foreclose questions about both the contexts which enable the practice of planning in the academy and the theories of practice which enable planning in the field. Current professional discursive and institutional hierarchies, however, authorize academic planners as privileged speakers within planning discourse.

From a poststructuralist perspective, it is no longer appropriate to assume that the search for a true or right way to plan is desirable or possible. Instead planning analysis can question the functions of various configurations of planning as they occur at particular sites—in academies, in journals, in public agencies, in private consulting firms. Concern with how planning is constituted within institutionalized practices can take the place of the quest for "the truth of the object" as an epistemological orientation within planning. Theorists are authorized to replace speculation about a unitary "planning" with questions about ways in which meaning in planning is produced. The level of inquiry moves from seeking the truth of planning to writing about how modes of planning discourse operate.

Current theories of planning often constitute planning in terms which exclude the non-academic contexts in which planning occurs. As a result types of planning which appear within academic discourse are opposed to and elevated above types of planning being produced at local bureaucratic sites. Another way to say this is to say that bureaucratic planning has been the excluded other within official planning theory.

This has been the case in different ways in both so-called rational theories of planning and in neo-Marxist theory. For example, Andreas Faludi's (1973) procedural planning is constructed in terms of an implicit liberal narrative. There is an implied tolerance for difference in his distinction between theories *of* planning and theories *in* planning. At the same time, however, he concentrates his authorial attention on (and hence authorizes) theories *of* planning.

Furthermore, Michael Ryan (1982: 124) points out how Faludi's reliance on universal rationality "provides a model for the further planned development of capitalism." Ryan argues that the "metaphysics" of Faludi's theory assumes the rationality of the individual subject—a "master planner," in effect—"a benign and friendly fascism" which excludes the complicity of planning theory in authorizing and enforcing a particular way of life. Ryan's analysis highlights "the marginalization of anything that puts the norm in question": in this case, consideration of the context within which rational planning must be exercised. This point is clear in federal programs such as the Housing Act of 1954, Section 701, The Housing Act of 1959, The Intergovernmental Cooperation Act of 1968, Urban Renewal, Community Action Programs, Model Cities, Comprehensive Health Planning, and "federal grant programs for planning in the realms of transportation, housing, open space, and environmental quality" (Brooks 1988: 243-244) which required planning and thus conditioned the terms of its practice. Faludi, of course, ignores this fundamental constitutive conditioning of planning practice defined by federal legislation, regulations, handbooks, memorandums, and discussions among program managers.

Rational planning is a de-contextualized theory, i.e., planning separated from all the structural and contingent realities such as the systems of exchange which characterize bureaucratic life in corporate democracy. There is a sense in which rational planning is a theological planning, which excludes practical politics and other external forces which enable the existence of the profession at all.

Neo-Marxist planning theory, on the other hand, privileges external forces and thus does contextualize planning, but in the service of promoting Marxism as an explanatory system and at the expense of local practices. The type of planning produced is created in the image of the Marxist meta-narrative. This is a powerful corrective to the decontextualization inherent in the rational models. But it works at the expense of not serving (and of not being of service) to analyze the production of meaning within the context of local practices in the academy and in the bureaucracy. So, for example, writing from an oppositional, Marxist position, Chris Paris recognizes that rational "theories of planning obscure . . . the relationship between the practice of planning and its social, economic and political context. That context in contemporary capitalist societies is the continuing dynamic of capital accumulation" (1982: 10). The liberal conceptual scheme which identifies planning with democratic choice is "traded in" for a another conceptual scheme which defines planning in terms of a predetermined theory of history. This move reifies modes of production, making them an objective reality which operates at a macro-level to structure reality. If rational planning is a planning of hope, Marxist planning is, in some respects, a planning of resignation. Neither invites investigation into the ebb and flow of the politics of planning as it is practiced in the context of ongoing struggles at the local level.

Because planning as it is practiced in the academy is the site both for training professional planners and for creating planning knowledge, academic planners are established as privileged speakers. While planning practitioners may complain that planning theory isn't relevant to bureaucratic planning, planners in the university often have the last word about the shape and preservation of the discipline. The fetish of concern about the separation between theory and practice traditionally has led to speculation about how planning practice fails to live up to the high moral tone of planning theory. Contemporary developments have been focused on planning practice and on participation in intra-disciplinary debate within the academy about which planning is the "real planning." A poststructuralist approach can direct analysis towards making the different representations of planning among planners in the academy and planners in the streets points for investigation. If privileged speakers are de-authorized, more voices can join the conversation.

4. The Practice of Theory and Theories of Practice

A poststructuralist thinker whose work is directly applicable to the problem of devising a mode of inquiry which moves beyond the automatic bifurcation of planning theory and planning practice is Michel Foucault.

Foucault (1984) has taken as his project in a number of cases the investigation of the "problematization" of acts, thoughts, and practices in terms of which meaning is generated at various institutionalized sites. In his study of sexuality, for example, he begins by discounting the notion of a single entity called sexuality and instead produces a genealogy of its formulation in the context of the requirements of an industrial order. More importantly, Foucault presents a model of analysis which is oriented towards questioning the relationship between forms of knowledge such as psychoanalytic discourse and the power exercised in related practices. In *Discipline and Punish*, he focuses on how the development of new forms of "scientific" knowledge were interrelated with new forms of discipline in the society. For Foucault, knowledge does not exist in the academy and practice on the streets. Instead knowledge and practice are interrelated in economies of reason. The model of the panopticon which he describes at length in *Discipline and Punish* becomes a model for analyzing forms of social order. We can imagine a number of panopticons divided along disciplinary lines, each constituting subjects in its own image in terms of the varying practices of any number of local sites. For Foucault, knowledge is not separate from power. We should expect to ask how the two are interwoven as the constitutive elements of modern discursive practices where ever they appear.

The disciplinary power that Foucault studies is productive, not merely repressive or oppressive. This means that discursive practices don't involve questions of liberation so much as questions about what forms of subjectivity are possible. This concern with the form of subjectivity requires him to explain the apparent shift from disciplinary practices in Volume I of *The History of Sexuality* to the production of the self in Volume II. Both continue a concern with the genealogies of forms of subjectivity.

The analysis of the constitution of the homeless within American political discourse provides a timely example of a Foucauldian approach to the politics of representation. Current pre-existing institutional practices, such as social work with authorized speakers, are participating in attempts to find the appropriate disciplinary categories with which to define the homeless. This is a definitional struggle which operates at the constitutive level. The homeless enter political discourse as decontextualized entities and/or, as they become the concern of these pre-existing professional practices, they are created in *disciplinary* terms: mentally ill, clients, criminals, deviants, etc. In this way the social and political relations that produce "the homeless" are not considered necessary to consider. This is particularly ironic because on the surface of the name we use in everyday life—"homeless"—is important information about the conditions which produced them. Specific policies of the Reagan administration which actually reduced the amount of available housing was a major contributing factor. But the decontextualization of the homeless—they spouted like dandelions on our collective lawn—allows the past and current administrations to express distress over "the plight of the homeless" and to brace themselves for the "hard choices" about the level of support that can be allocated, given the other worthy cases which also need attention, without taking any blame for prior bad planning.

Similarly, the conventional split between theory and practice in planning decontextualizes both. In the office, planning does not operate without a theory of practice (regardless of the fact that most theorists have not deemed to notice). In the academy planning does not operate in a void free from institutionalized practices (regardless of loose talk about academics being separated from any real world concerns). The task for planning criticism is to develop theories of practice and recognize how practice conditions the formulation of theory. This task can illuminate the function of the customary theory/practice split and allow us to assess its contribution to "the current crisis" involving the promise and the products of planning that Dykeman articulated so clearly.

5. The Practice of Theory

Existing histories of planning theory often suggest an implicit Kuhnian structure showing shifts from The City Beautiful to Functional Planning to Comprehensive Planning to Economic Development Planning and Public-Private Partnerships. These histories are useful for locating events sequentially, but they exclude other considerations which are central to understanding the practice of theory as an academic discipline. As several commentators suggest, the Kuhnian notion of paradigm shift does not include forces outside of disciplines because Kuhn is concerned with the meaning of paradigm shift for what is considered respectable knowledge inside a discipline. He is alert to internal power struggles in a way that de-emphasizes external forces on a discipline. Similarly, the familiar view of planning history needs to be supplemented with a genealogical view. That would mean asking not about the shifts inside theories, as if no practical considerations were involved, but rather asking what practical agendas may have been operating in the generation of theoretical shifts.

A Kuhnian approach to studying planning theory would emphasize syntagmatic relations, i.e., how meaning is produced within systems. This would lead to research into shifts in the rules of internal organization to explain transformations in planning theory. In contrast, Marxist analysis would focus on paradigmatic relations, that is, how external forces condition planning. This approach would focus on outside pressures on planning. A poststructuralist approach to planning combines syntagmatic and paradigmatic approaches. Analysis would focus on interpreting how syntagmatic and paradigmatic relations intersect to produce meaning. To take this perspective is to ask how external forces are represented in the familiar rules for constituting planning theory. In other words, poststructuralism is a mode of inquiry at the meta-theoretical level: what kinds of planning theory are possible? How are the conventions produced that allow theory to continue in acceptable and understandable forms?

This approach is easier to apply to planning practiced in non-academic settings, partly because of the Marxist tradition in urban studies. Thus it is not surprising to learn that in cities where political regimes give priority to developmental goals, planning departments will produce different analyses of problems and different policy recommendations than in cities where regimes are committed to redistributive goals.

But the politics of representation which condition planning theory in academic settings can also be studied. For example, in the preface to *Restructuring the City*, Susan and Norman Fainstein (1983) include the usual disclaimer: the study was funded by HUD; the book does not represent the official views of the United States government. Then they do something not so typical which illustrates the kinds of issues poststructural analyses of planning theory pursue. The authors include the information that they severed their relations with HUD when they were prohibited from publishing their findings without prior clearance. Interpretation of how this type of influence conditions the production of knowledge within planning is deauthorized by approaches to theory which unproblematically accept the identity of planning with methods based on instrumental rationality. A poststructuralist approach begins with the assumption that planning theory is produced in the play between authorized value (external forces) and approved methods (internal grammar) and then goes on to investigate how that process works.

A major agenda item of planning since the Second World War has been the establishment of planning within the university and within the state bureaucracy. To read the planning theory of this era is to read over and over again "Conclusion and Implications" sections that call for more planning. Thus even the formulation of comprehensive planning was conditioned by concerns with establishing planning as a recognized discipline within the academy. Part of this process required differentiating planning from other disciplines: planning is not architecture and certainly not landscape architecture. Part of the process established claims to intellectual respectability: i.e., planning methodology is based on the same scientific methodology by which social sciences such as sociology are identified. Subsequent challenges to comprehensive planning can be seen as similarly conditioned by paradigmatic relations: both by shifts in the epistemology of the social sciences which authorize the rationality claims of comprehensive planning and by reports from the field about the irrationality of planning practice.

6. Theories of Practice

Planning in professional settings also entails the production of meaning in the inter-play between syntagmatic and paradigmatic codes. Analysis of the politics of representation places planning practice in the context of American corporate democracy. The theory of planning practice needs to account for voters as well as the influence of professional training. Case studies of planning practices are useful for unraveling how professional techniques are generated in the context of public and private agencies. Asking whether or not planning "succeeds" is misleading; instead, planning criticism can focus on how planning has performed at the constitutive level and seek to generalize about that. Three historically relevant areas of concern are the insertion of planning as a taken for granted segment of city administration, the actualization of planning methods in terms of local and temporal contingencies, and the relationship of particular instances of planning practices to other powerful discursive practices, such as legal discourse or a strong political regime.

There is some evidence that acceptance of planning professionals within the public sector was negotiated at the cost of the ability to effect plans. This limitation, the price of admission, in other words, helps to insure that the foundational structuring of the society around accumulation of wealth continues undisturbed and is even reproduced. One example of how planning has avoided challenging the current political economy is the tendency within dominant planning theories to identify liberal democracy on the basis of choice (freedom) rather than on the basis of social justice (equality). Minority positions such as advocacy planning which are concerned with distributive issues flourish in the context of the university, not in professional settings. When planning has had a powerful effect on urban policy, it is in instances when particular planning departments or politically astute "master planners" have been promoted by and allied with other powerful discursive practices, such as legal discourse or a popular centralized political regime.

7. Current Events in Theories of Practice and the Practice of Planning

There is a current move within planning theory to produce studies of planning practice. This move has been organized to large extent by Howell Baum and includes, among others, Charles Hoch (1988) and John Forester (1988). The movement is based in part on a reading of critical theorists such as Habermas and on poststructuralists such as Foucault. I will argue below that these are idiosyncratic readings which by their partiality and mistaken claims about representing a new synthesis illuminate the function of the continuing bifurcation of theory and practice within the discipline. In other words, instead of ending the representation of planning in terms of the theory/practice split, the current fashion of research into practice re-enforces it.

John Forester's emphasis on developing a code of ethics for practicing planners is an example of one form of the move within the academy to recognize planning practice (Forester 1988). In an ongoing study of Norman Krumholz's tenure as Planning Director of Cleveland, Forester presents an idealized narrative of planning practice in a hortatory rather than analytic mode. Forester's work de-emphasizes analysis at the level of discourse in favor of fostering a belief in undistorted communication as the basis for an ethical program for planners. Similarly, Hoch (1988) makes the case for "free spaces" in planning. If language not only carries meaning, but constitutes it, then the production of meaning is always contextual. This impugns the notion of undistorted communication as Forester has adapted it from Habermas' work. At the least, "dialogue" is possible only within communities of shared values. The ideal speech situation can more usefully be thought of as a kind of idealized other, rather than as an empirical situation.

So in a way similar to rational planning tradition, notions of undistorted communication or free spaces are schemes that mirror our hopes. They represent an ideological position about what a good society and good planning should be. Such representations aren't anthropological, so much as reflections on the shortcomings of our way of life. In other words, the hopes for community embodied in proposals for a planning theory of practice are produced by modern life. In a related project, to outline an ethical program for planning, Hoch (1988: 29) reads Foucault in terms of "liberating the individual." This interprets Foucault's concerns with the subject in a way which "forgets" Foucault's epistemological roots in contemporary language theory. Foucault sees disciplinary power as productive. There is less an oppressed individual waiting to be liberated in the disciplinary society than the need to question what forms of subject are possible. Hoch's interpretation turns him away from attending to the contexts within which planners in professional settings work, and he only calls for planning practice of limited types.

Both Forester and Hoch repeat and supplement the historical call in planning theory for more planning without being self-reflective about the implications of this project. They re-enforce the desire for a unitary planning theory whose privileged speakers are based in the academy. As suggested above, this is accomplished in part by de-emphasizing the economic and political context which produces them as university planners and which generates the conditions of professional planning practice. The implicit promotion of the establishment of planning as a discipline has been transformed into a justification for planning theory as an intellectual/moral activity. This operates against the pressure that planning education be constituted as technical training for establishment functionaries and also against a shifting occupational structure and structure of public support that finds planning at least superfluous and at most an obstruction in the orderly growth mode of current development. The function of the current form of the theory/practice split is to justify the position of planning as it is practiced in the academy. The irony of the current turn to research in practice in planning theory, at least in the two examples discussed above, is that it has less to do with developing theories of practices and more to do with insuring the practice of theory.

8. In Conclusion: Some Implications of the Theory/Practice Split for the Politics of Planning

Two curious planning related documents appeared in the first quarter of 1989: the Brooks et al. debate, cited in the first section of this essay, speculating on the purpose of planning; and a column by William Raspberry in *The Washington Post* suggesting a new urban policy. While reputedly about the future of planning, the Brooks article has led to an academic discussion over modes of representing the history of planning. Meanwhile William Raspberry has entered a plea for using military troops— either the National Guard which has the advantage of being made up of local residents or the regular army which has the advantage of experience with loaded weapons—to restore minimal order to certain Washington, D.C. neighborhoods.

That's the East Coast. We can also turn to the West Coast to ask whether the foregoing discussion was merely an interesting intellectual exercise or whether it has anything to do with Dykeman's notion that current crises in planning are tied to the split between theory and practice. An earlier version of this discussion was presented to the 29th Annual Conference of the Association of Collegiate Schools of Planning in Los Angeles in 1988. At that time my notion of the current crisis in planning had to do with our presence in The Biltmore, a lovingly restored hotel, and the fact that before my panel I had taken a walk around the neighborhood outside and had stepped around young men sleeping on the sidewalk.

These young men are the victims of a theoretical, administrative, and economic "space" of contemporary urban forms which are organized to facilitate global exchange. The organization produces a "political economy of social dislocation" (Dear 1986: 380). What I take this to mean is that activities which do not contribute to the development of advanced capitalism are excluded from the discourse of planning theorists and practioners. That exclusion affects people whose occupational training is linked to manufacturing housing that is not tailored to the new professional class. They, too, are excluded and economic activities that support these dislocated forms and other alternative practices are relegated to the status of the "illegal"—or at least considered irregular forms of social and economic and cultural life.

This alternative form of theorizing, of recognizing dislocation, links events that conventional policy discussions consider separately. Conventional theory defines: 1) homelessness as a social welfare problem, 2) the drug culture as a criminal problem, and 3) local informal economies flourishing outside of official channels as blackmarkets. These and other characteristics of contemporary cities are not separate types of problems as they appear to be when they are placed in different discursive realms. They are all produced by the "political economy of social dislocation" that results from the privileged use of urban space for exchange relations which are globally oriented rather than only site specific.

A metaphor for the contemporary urban form is postmodern architecture in the urban fortress style such as the Peachtree Plaza in Atlanta and the Bonaventure in Los Angeles or "mega-structures" in general. These buildings work by offering an equivalent or substitution for the city. Fredric Jameson (1984) suggests that the Heideggian opposition between the world and nature has been displaced in late capitalism by an opposition between the world and our technological representation of it. Thus, within the urban fortress all the valorized life is inside: hanging gardens, shops, restaurants, conventions centers, rooms for temporary stays. All the city is outside—excluded: the beggars in the streets, the vendors, the weather, time, space, and social relations as we know them in everyday life. The social disintegration that Raspberry notes is only one indicator of the larger problem not only of incidental populations but also of incidental cities where the urban space itself has become a barrier to exchange.

Planning theorists in the academy will miss the practical human implications of their participation in the adaptation of the city to the global economy to the extent that they continue to argue about whether rational planning should be taught as if it existed or whether theorists should be engaged in defining a unitary ethic for practitioners. Planning practitioners will be implicated in their own representations of planning which displace the city and its inhabitants to the extent that they ignore the theoretical underpinnings of their world.

This is a much revised version of a paper presented to the John Dyckman Memorial Panel at the 29th Annual conference of the Collegiate Schools of Planning in Los Angeles, November 1988. I would like to thank David Perry and Dennis Crow for comments they made on earlier versions of this paper.

References

Brooks, Michael P. (1988). "Four Critical Junctures in the History of the Urban Planning Profession: An Exercise in Hindsight." *Journal of the American Planning Association*, (Spring): 241-248.

Bourdieu, Pierre. (1977). *Outline of a Theory of Practice*, Cambridge: Cambridge University Press.

Cisneros, Henry. (1989). "Have Planners Taken Their Eye off the Ball?" *Journal of the American Planning Association*, (Winter): 78-79.

Boyer, M. Christine. (1983). *Dreaming the Rational City*. Cambridge, MA: MIT Press.

Bryson, Norman. (1981). *Work and Image: French Painting of the Ancien Regime*. Cambridge: Cambridge University Press.

Checkoway, Barry, ed. (1986). *Strategic Perspectives on Planning Practice*. Lexington, MA: Lexington Books.

Corlett, William S. (1987). "Taking Time Out For Community: The Political Implications of Derrida." Presented at the 83rd meeting of the American Political Science Association (Foundations of Political Theory Section), Palmer House and Towers, Chicago, IL, September 3-6.

Dear, M. J. (1986). "Postmodernism and Planning." *Society and Space*, 4: 367-384.

———— and Allen J. Scott, eds. (1981). *Urbanization and Urban Planning in Capitalist Society*. London: Methuen.

de Man, Paul. (1983). *Blindness and Insight*. Minneapolis: University of Minnesota Press.

Dyckman, John. (1978). "Three Crises of American Planning: Planning, Professionalism, and the University." *Planning Theory in the 1980's: A Search for Future Directions*. Eds. Robert W. Burchell and George Sternlieb. New Brunswick, NJ: Center for Urban Policy.

Fainstein, Susan S. and Norman I. Fainstein. (1988). *Restructuring the City*. New York: Longman.

Faludi, Andreas, ed. (1973). *A Reader in Planning Theory*. New York: Pergamon Press.

Fogelsong, Richard E. (1986). *Planning the Capitalist City*. Princeton, NJ: Princeton University Press.

Forester, John. (1988). "Evaluation, Persistence, Traps and Possibilities." Presented to the 30th Annual Conference of the Association of Collegiate Schools of Planning, Buffalo, NY, October 27-30.

Foucault, Michel. (1977). *Discipline and Punish*. New York: Pantheon Books.

————. (1984). "Polemics, Politics, and Problemizations." *The Foucault Reader*. Ed. Paul Rabinow. New York: Pantheon.

Hoch, Charles. (1988). "A Pragmatic Inquiry." *Transaction: Social Science and Modern Society*, 26 (1): 27-35.

Jameson, Fredric. (1984). "Postmodernism, or The Cultural Logic of Late Capitalism." *New Left Review*, 146: 53-92.

Marcuse, Peter. (1989). "Who/What Decides What Planners Do?" *Journal of the American Planning Association*, (Winter): 79-81.

Milroy, Beth Moore. (1988). "Constructing and Deconstructing Plausibility." Unpublished typescript.

Paris, Chris, ed. (1982). *Critical Readings in Planning Theory*. New York: Pergamon Press.

Ryan, Michael. (1982). *Marxism and Deconstruction*. Baltimore: Johns Hopkins University Press.

Raspberry, William. (1989). "Call out the Troops." *The Washington Post*. Weekly Edition, 6 (17): 29.

Said, Edward. (1978). *Orientalism*. New York: Random House.

Teitz, Michael B. (1989). "The Uses and Misuses of History." *Journal of the American Planning Association*, (Winter): 81-82.

Weiss, Marc A. (1989). "Planning History: What Story? What Meaning? What Future?" *Journal of the American Planning Association*, (Winter): 82-84.

The narrative of architecture, urban planning, and economic development in Washington, D.C.   *(photo by Dennis Crow)*

> We must invent and rebuild *ex novo* our Modern City like an immense and tumultous shipyard, active, mobile, and everywhere dynamic, and the modern building like a giant machine.[1]

Le Corbusier's

Post-Modern

Plan

Dennis Crow, AICP

U.S. Dept. of Housing and Urban Development

LE CORBUSIER'S *The City of Tomorrow and Its Planning* is usually interpreted as one of the most important documents of modernism and as one of the most dominant guides to "rational" urban design. In the literature of planning history, both architectural and planning theorists have interpreted it as a great attempt to justify a scientific approach to solving urban problems. Similarly, in the U. S., the creation of the disciplines of public administration, political science, and urban planning focused on solving problems of urban sanitation, housing, and traffic as well as the reform of municipal government. The traditional training of urban planners was based on the assumption that "politics" must be excluded from administration, and only the "scientific" study of problems could produce the best result. This training in public administration and urban planning shared the assumptions of philosophical modernism about the supremacy of science over art, technique over politics, and reason over affect.

In this discussion, I am concerned with the way Le Corbusier fails to maintain these distinctions and hierarchies, particularly that of planning and politics. In his attempts to justify the technical approach to urban planning, one would expect Le Corbusier to use and argue for a scientific and comprehensive approach to solving urban problems. Indeed, he emphatically calls for that. However, his argument for the "scientific investigation" of cities and its application to urban problems is constantly at odds with his other signifying strategies. The verbal text consists mostly of two sets of arguments for the "scientific investigation" of cities, which I discuss below. The graphic text has a "rhetoric" that seems only to reinforce them. His work employs the latest technology of its day, but looks like the most "post-modern" texts available now. In showing that, I also attempt to show that Le Corbusier's work challenges the distinction between modernism and post-modernism by providing a reading of the verbal and graphic texts of the work which questions any attempt to place it in either modern or post-modern periods of philosophical history. So what is the relationship between politics and planning and the post-modernism question? To address that question, we must consider three related issues: (1) text and image in the book, (2) the blank frame and the plan, and (3) questioning the post-modern frame in architecture and planning. I want to signal a developing transition in my argument that hinges on the association of the terms planning, science, and modernism and on their asymmetrical counterparts: politics, art, and post-modernism. The point being that within Le Corbusier's pinnacle text of modernism those oppositions cannot be sustained.

Le Corbusier's book reads and was no doubt written like a comprehensive plan, but the realization of his argument is undermined by what urban planners were once trained to believe are extraordinary or extraneous, irrational, incidental, or unfortunate elements of the planning process. Those elements take Le Corbusier's plan of the book and the plan of the city in unexpected directions. All the ways by which textual strategies (e.g., figures, tropes, examples, classifications, and, in this case, drawings, photos, and newspaper clippings) contribute to and exceed the meaning of any argument are like the ways in which politics contributes to and exceeds the technical aspirations of planning. Moreover, planning and politics are, in large part, the work of those textual strategies. In the end, Le Corbusier's work does not reveal a guide for rational town planning, but leaves only a blank space—an open zone which like the so-called free market receives its determination by the exercise of public and private power.

1. The Text/Image Frame of Le Corbusier's
The City of Tomorrow and its Planning

Le Corbusier presents two arguments for his concept of planning, and those arguments represent very well philosophical modernism. They appear to justify a "rational" approach to solving urban problems through the use of geometry, statistics, engineering, and business administration. However, those arguments which depend on textual strategies for their appearance as arguments are contested by the use of other signifying strategies; in the same manner, the graphic text has a similarly contadictory structure. Le Corbusier attempts to use photographs, drawings, and renderings to establish oppositions between science and art, poetry and technique, reason and emotion, etc. Like other writers of his time, he hopes to demolish these oppositions in order to realize some vague synthesis of them. The images are not merely illustrations of particular points in his argument. The photographs, clippings, drawings, and architectural renderings partially reflect, while serving to undermine, the epistemological hierarchy Le Corbusier takes for granted. Two of the most important images, the blank "frame" and the painting at the end of the translated texts, undermine his argument in a distinctly post-modern way, and reveal a point more indicative than Le Corbusier's point of what might pass for post-modern thinking about cities.

Le Corbusier (1982: 1) begins with the assertion that "A town is a tool." The "tool" or "frame" for presenting his argument would seem to be that of the technical tools of planning: mapping, statistical research, drafting, substantive engineering, and legal knowledge coupled with imagination.[2] Through all the strategies he uses to construct and privilege geometry, science, and technique against poetry, art, and politics, these seemingly "marginalized" elements not only slip through his grid of argument but also overpower it.

Le Corbusier has two major sets of arguments. One is a philosophical argument based on ideas about the mind, geometry, nature, anatomy, and physiology. The other is an argument about the historical and demographic changes in European cities, specifically the rapid population growth of cities in the late nineteenth century and about the congestion and pollution caused by new technology, principally the automobile. Le

Corbusier wants to discover exactly how the development of a city takes place and to find a "formula which should give the rules on which modern town planning must rest." However, he ends with an invocation of premodern history and the absolutist state—a point I shall return to in the conclusion of this discussion.

The first argument is based on the primacy of geometry for perception, cognition, and building. He opens the book by stating, "Geometry is the means, created by ourselves, whereby we perceive the external world and express the world within us. Geometry is the foundation." This is the peak of Le Corbusier's epistemological hierarchy. He identifies what he takes to be the foundation of knowledge with what is first, essential, and the highest. However, within this assertion lies a logical transgression of categories of the *a priori* and *a posteriori*, and, asymmetrically, of nature and culture, which Jacques Derrida (1978a) exposes in his introduction to Husserl's *Origin of Geometry*. To simplify Derrida's question, we might ask here how we (humanity) could have created a foundation within us on which we stand. That becomes a riddle of phenomenology and history which Le Corbusier ignores and which, according to Derrida, Husserl was unable to untangle. The basis for its application to cities is contained in the following caption or slogan: "The right angle is the essential and sufficient implement of action, because it enables us to determine space with an absolute exactness" (Le Corbusier 1982: 19). The result of its application is the cadestral plan that determines space as well as property. Because Le Corbusier presupposes that geometry is prior to experience and reason, its posterior realization through building is privileged. The more cities mirror geometry, the more privileged they are in the hierarchy of "civilization." He writes (1982: 43), "Where the orthogonal is supreme, there we read the height of a civilization." The etymological root, "ortho," means straight and upright. The word "read" here marks the logical priority and privilege of vision as well as a pre-critical notion of writing. This conjunction of ideas about geometry, vision, and reading allows him to pull together other techniques of drawing, building, and writing through the grids of analytic geometry, the squares of graphs, tables, and charts, and the city blocks of land-use maps.

The modern city Le Corbusier defines by the presence of straight lines. He states (1982: 16), "A modern city lives by the straight line, inevitably; for the construction of buildings, sewers and tunnels, highways, pavements. The circulation of traffic demands the straight line; it is the proper thing for the heart of a city." The model urban renewal plan which conforms to the straight line is, for Le Corbusier and other planners, Baron von Hausmann's reconstruction of the boulevards of Paris. Through demolition and reconstruction, Hausmann wanted to "cut a cross north to south and east to west, through the center of Paris, bringing the city's cardinal points into direct communication" (Choay 1969). According to Le Corbusier, the purpose of architecture is to bring together the "products of passion" (poetry) and the "products of reason" (engineering) according to the "standards of mechanical beauty." Given the dictates of geometry, the latter transforms the former. Le Corbusier writes that the purpose of "town planning" is to analyze the city through "scientific investigation" (1982: 72). The "cross" that marks the city becomes interchangeable with the cross formed by lines of graphs and statistical charts (Le Corbusier 1982: 106-122). Perhaps with some irony, Le Corbusier writes (1982: 126), "statistics are merciless things."

The last chapter, "Finance and Realization," is almost more important than the details of the Voisin Plan. Le Corbusier opens the chapter with a caption which he certifies to have become a "stereotype" in 1922: "But where is the money coming from?" This has become a cliché repeated in every undergraduate planning course today. It is important here for two reasons. First, it is indicative of the strict limitations of urban planning in an economic or political context which narrowly defines and enforces individual property rights. Second, in keeping with the long-standing understanding of the constraints of interpreting of laws governing individual property rights, he recommends the creation of business plazas in central city areas. Those plazas would contain housing for residence owners, small business, cafes, shops, open spaces, and office towers (Le Corbusier 1982: 245-247). These developments would be financed by U.S., British, German, and Japanese capital.

If one is in an historical frame of mind, Le Corbusier's anticipation of the "post-industrial" city would not go unnoticed. Read in light of the "revitalization" or "redevelopment" of inner-city areas now, his plan for what are called Mixed Use Developments in the U. S. means condominiums, specialty shops, downtown shopping malls, theaters, restaurants, and (concrete) parks. Large multi-use developments such as the IDS Building in Minneapolis, Rockefellar Center in New York,

Greenway Plaza in Houston, One Main Place in Dallas, One Mellon Plaza in Pittsburgh, and, ironically, L'Enfant Plaza in Washington, D.C. (where I work for the U.S. Dept. of Housing and Urban Development) illustrate Le Corbusier's plans well. All that is missing is reference to the circulation of capital from the Persian Gulf states, Hong Kong by way of Canada, and France. However, he is implicitly aware of the problems of capital flight and the weakness of municipal government which prohibit the creation of such centers for public purposes in European and U.S. cities. With these examples in mind, one might write an architectural history in which this is alternatively interpreted as the destruction or realization of reason in planning, or of the end of modernism or the beginning of post-modernism. Placing Le Corbusier in such histories becomes harder rather than easier. Yet it is not Le Corbusier that presents that difficulty. It is the writing of architectural history and criticism that is the source of the problem. I, however, have chosen to address the philosophical, rather than historical, issues which confound the debates about post-modernism. At this point, however, it is gratuitous to work the chiasmus that writing the history of architecture becomes implicitly, but necessarily, a writing of an architecture for history.

Le Corbusier ends the book with a discussion of his role in creating the Voisin Plan for Paris. He claims (1982: 298) that he is only taking a technical, not a political role. In this work and in the earlier *Towards a New Architecture*, he dissociates himself from the Bolshevik Party and the "left" in general, and asserts his purity as a technician, writing in the role of the technician. He apologizes for not providing more "figures" that would substantiate his technical expertise. He writes, "My book is lacking in figures, and it is a great pity. . . . Figures are all important, I know." If we read the book as a technical work, we would assume that he means statistics, tables, graphs, charts, and architectural drawings.

The double meaning of "figure," however, should not go unanalyzed. If one reads "figures" as statistics, one might agree that a "scientific investigation" of urban demographics requires more information than charts on migration and cartoons about traffic accidents. If one reads "figures" as "figures of speech" and broadens that to include signifying strategies in general, one sets in motion an inquiry into Le Corbusier's use of "rhetoric," classification, citation, examples, etc., which are far from the "technical" expertise of architects and planners. The images

throughout the book are "figures" in this sense. Even the table of geo-
metrical "figures" (1982: 8), by being cited as a "common-place" book,
or primer, for architects becomes a symbol for the "scientific investigation"
of cities. Its appearance in the book invites analysis of the "origin of
geometry."

The graphic text of *The City of Tomorrow and Its Planning* consists
of reproductions of photographs, architectural renderings, free-hand
drawings, a pallet of geometric forms copied from students' text books,
photomontages, collages of drawings, reproductions of postcards, reproductions of cartoons from newspapers, graphs, charts, and reproductions
of paintings (one of which is blank). Each chapter is also introduced with
captions or slogans printed on a single page. Those slogans are contained
in the following chapter sometimes with, and sometimes without, alteration.
Data and diagrams have a figurative role in this text as well. These figures
compose a "revelatory collage"[3] which is folded into the argument, but
exceeds it at every turn.

There are two general points to be made without taking time to analyze
each image separately. First, ironically the most advanced technology
of visual reproduction at that time, photography, is used to document
the congestion and misery of cities. Photography is used in every instance
to signal the conditions of the least architecturally advanced cities. Detailed
perspective drawings are used for representations of advanced cities of
the future. One could simply state that photography is the most graphic
means for documenting actual conditions and drawing is the only way
to represent the future. This bit of "common sense" should not be allowed
to overpower the observation that Le Corbusier's use of these methods
parallels his epistemological hierarchy. That is, the more the geometry
of cities stands out, the better they are. Therefore, photography is better
suited to represent the seamy side of cities.

The textual strategies of these images can be seen in the following
examples. The *The City of Tomorrow* opens with photos of "A London
Suburb" that symbolizes what planning should replace. Photographs of
London, Paris, New York, Vienna, Venice, and other cities are used
throughout to symbolize the dismal qualities of existing residential areas
or anachronistic architecture. The only exceptional use of photography
is the pictures of airplanes, automobiles, metros, ships, dams, and the
interior of one "modern" house. The house was built by Le Corbusier

before 1926. These objects are obscure symbols for the speed and complexity to be achieved with cities through planning. The architectural renderings have clean, precise lines illustrating plans for buildings and cities. The photo-montages juxtapose the two, combining a photo with an architectural rendering.

In spite of the planning of visual information in the text, its clarity is compromised, or undermined, by the use of photographic reproductions of postcards. Le Corbusier (1982: 53, 123) includes reproductions of postcards of Paris in the text. One celebrates Paris without automobiles. Someone (Le Corbusier?) has written over it: "Il ne pas une auto, 1909." The other is entitled "Paris at the start of the 20th. Century" and is dated 1908. The Eiffel Tower, a Ferris wheel, and a dirigible appear as the symbols of the century. On the following page there is another photograph of a Ferris wheel which is accompanied by the caption, "Here is the age of steel; an age of confusion . . . Lyricism and the poetry of mathematics . . . but by 1920 the Great Wheel no longer existed; the verdict had been passed and an idol overthrown." These machines symbolize the precision and speed Le Corbusier envisioned for cities as a whole. However, the complexity and diversity of these images invite interpretation that may contradict the hierarchy for which he attempts to argue.

In his review of Derrida's *The Post Card*, Gregory Ulmer (1981: 4) writes, "Identity, in all its aspects (truth and being) is the ideology of the postal principal . . . the post card circulates, its message exposed to anyone who looks, but, whether because of the excess or the poverty of the message, it is meaningless (without interest) to all, even to the signer and the recipient, who understand it to say no more than 'I am here.'" This statement is readily applicable to Le Corbusier's use of postcards. The postcard's effect, in *The City of Tomorrow and Its Planning*, is to represent the site of modernism; to create a location for it. Le Corbusier, as the signer of the postcards, can claim to have been there. Therefore, the postcards might be sent from sites, or periods, which he can claim are modern to sites which are pre-modern and anachronistic. Today, when he sends them to us, their pastiche of pre-modern and modern symbols and addresses makes them seem achronistic: out of time, either pre- or post-modern. Upon analysis the spatial and temporal demarcation of "modernism" begins to give way.

The identity of the scene of modernism and its site is compromised in two ways. First, the site is "Paris," which represents nearly all of European architectural history and the most graphic methods of "modern" town planning (those methods span the time from the 1850's until the present). Second, Le Corbusier draws attention to the technology, not the plan of the city, as the mark of its modernity. With the exception of the dirigible, the technology used to represent modernism is a product of the invention of cast-iron techniques and steel fabrication of the nineteenth century. The issue here is not the historical context of Le Corbusier's travels in and out of modernism. The ideology of the periodization of the pre- and post-modern is at issue. Though much of Derrida's arguments about the postal principle might be applicable here, I want to switch from concerns about creating periods according to classes of technology to analyzing the hidden "economism" of those classifications.

The second major point to be made about the visual information is that it nearly makes the verbal text superfluous. One could "read" the book without reading the two sets of arguments for the "rational-comprehensive" definition of urban planning. The images require the style of reading applicable to collage, cinema, or video art. Le Corbusier is using an experimental visual technology to seemingly support his arguments. However, reading this way requires one to manage fragmentation and discontinuity in order to arrive at meanings that seem to conform to the arguments. In this sense, Le Corbusier's use of visual technology contradicts his claims about the logical and perceptual priority of regular geometric figures and order. In addition, the images are symbols for, not examples of, his arguments about cities. His use of these symbols creates a texture different from that of the philosophical and demographic arguments, which comprise the written portion of the book. In a post-modern moment, the visual technology overpowers the arguments—to their detriment.

2. The Blank Frame and the Plan

Le Corbusier's use of many kinds of "figures," especially the gesture of apologizing for their absence, raises questions about what kind of text *The City of Tomorrow and Its Planning* actually is. It becomes less and less clear what kind of text it is, when it is, and what it means. In many ways, its organization is clearly post-modern. According to criteria offered by Palmer (1979), Owens (1980), Lyotard (1984), Jameson (1983), and Ulmer (1983, 1985), it meets many different criteria. It has a quality of being "beyond" metaphysics and time, it has non-narrative strategies for advancing ideas, it is constructed as a pastiche of images, and it contains a concluding and encompassing allegory. The entire text can be read as an allegory for the comprehensive planning process whereby planning is replaced by economics, technique by politics, and science by art. There are two powerful images that undo those ideas of technical planning: "scientific investigation," and the distinctly "modern" plan for urban development. Those images, the blank frame and the allegory of the plan and its politics, are the concern of this section.

Le Corbusier is concerned about the timeliness of his work. He writes, (1982: 88) "A feeling is in the air, a sort of general assent to a group of new and opportune doctrines." He claims that the evolving spirit makes new claims on ideas and technology, and is ready to transform the city. This transformation is the result of a "modern spirit, this irresistible force, overflowing and uncontrollable now, but [is] derived from the slow efforts of our forefathers" (1982: 45). The enthusiastic attempt to describe the time and spirit lead only to a blank page (1982: 39).

Here only a blank page appears with a rectangle drawn in the upper half of the page. Inside the rectangle is the phrase, "Left blank for a work expressing modern feeling." Ironically, the page which is not blank is made blank by the inscription on it of the phrase "left blank." The frame circumscribes this new spirit only by keeping out all that is in the text which is not new. This is an empty center which somehow excludes everything but something for which there is no example. Perhaps, the frame itself—that textual strategy of exclusion, regulation, administration, engineering—is the signifier Le Corbusier would like to stand for "modern feeling." It is placed in the book as though it should be always available for the most current example to be selected by any reader at any time (any "modern" time?). The blank frame could only be filled by citation of some other representation of a "feeling." What is impossible to determine is whether the blank frame is a supplement to the text or vice versa. The blank frame is like a vacant parcel of land which is constantly appreciating in price. The discovery of the blank spot begins the process of urban development. However, the selection of something to represent that "feeling" or the value of that land is not the result of planning or technique, but of economics and politics.

What now pass for the themes in post-structuralist criticism of presence and absence or inclusion and exclusion could be taken up here. In preparation for comments by Gayatri Spivak in this regard, I would just cite a passage from Derrida's *The Truth of Painting*. In this work, Derrida writes of the picture, the mat, and the frame:

> This picture can, moreover, on occasion be replaced there by another which slides into the *passe-partout* as an 'example.' In this respect, the *passe-partout* remains a basically mobile structure; but while allowing something to appear, it does not form, nevertheless, *stricto sensu* a frame, within a frame . . . on its internal border properly speaking, and the external border of what it displays, allows or makes appear in its empty center: the image, tableau, figure, form, the system of lines and colors. (cited by Ulmer 1985: 109)

Le Corbusier's blank frame invites continuous commentary on the issues of citations, examples, borders, and margins. It seems to represent, on the one hand, a "modern" approach to breaking with the past in art and politics. It suggests that he cannot keep up with the speed of artistic and political change. It also suggests that any expression would become instantly anachronistic, and therefore always inadequate. The blank frame could only be adequate if something external to it certified any substitutions of its content to be "authentic" representations of "modern feeling." On the other hand, it represents the post-modern condition of infinite substitutability of images for art and politics. Nothing could stop this process. The blank frame represents only this process of shifting inclusion and exclusion. Another overlooked word for this is subalternation. Unable to control this process for the writing of *The City of Tomorrow and Its Planning*, Le Corbusier uses every available means of representation while, each time, he makes the concept of representation problematic. Furthermore, he appears to finish the work of representation by the invocation of political authority, and not by exercise of technique.

He provides another very important image about planning that fits into this blank frame. The book ends with the citation of a painting honoring Louis XIV, "the first Western townplanner since the Romans" (1982:

45).[4] The painting depicts Louis XIV gathering architects and engineers in the countryside in order to break ground for the building of the Invalides. The group of men and a horse are in the foreground, the valley and hills on the horizon are in the background, and an angel floats overhead pointing a trumpet at the men. The center of the painting, toward which all gestures of the the men and the action of the painting point, is the "plan" for "L'Hostel Royal des Invalides." The gestures of Louis XIV, the angel, and others point to the "plan," which is only a floor plan of the building outlined on a scroll. But there is much more to this painting.

The site for the building is suburban, removed from the central city which is on the horizon. The city and another village are rendered marginal to the available land. A man in the lower left hand corner, who seems to be pleading with the group, is a peasant or farmer protesting with the title or contract for this land in his hand. All the other gestures indicate he is being ignored. Most of the surrounding crowd is looking at Louis XIV, who is pointing to the floor plan. The painting is about him "commanding" the building of the retreat. That is, it is about commanding, not about planning. The word, "Plan," stands out underneath the outline of the building. The movement of the painting circulates toward the word, "plan." But there is no plan.

The accompanying caption and the textual reference are about Le Corbusier's "admiration" for this "great town planner." Louis XIV's ability to "conceive immense projects and realize them" clearly depends on his monarchial authority, and not his technical skills as a planner. It is important to notice that Le Corbusier notes his ability to command, as though that were sufficient to compel obedience on the part of architects. That authority is more easily exercised against "nature" in this suburban area were there may be cooperative large property owners and no opposing merchants to interfere. Only "nature," the restless horse, looks away. In short, this painting is not "about" architecture or planning, but is an allegory on the use of political authority to "get things done."

The painting is a rhetorical exercise in honoring this authority. But it is an allegory of the planning process as well. It seems to be a portrait of an event, but it is a narrative of a process. The "modern" planning process which he allegorizes, involves finding a site for building, doing the architectural drafting, buying the land, and exercising the political authority to organize the financing and labor to construct the building.

All of this is to be accomplished by ignoring adversely effected citizens and dominating "nature." Until recently, this has been thought of as the ideal, frictionless process of implementing urban planning, and often still seems to be the model for private-sector land development. This preconceived supremacy of political and administrative authority defines the "modern" desire in the early days of planning theory. Le Corbusier acknowledges that political authority, rather than technique, is fundamental to planning when he proclaims in the 1947 preface that ". . . town planning really becomes as it were, the mirror of authority and, it may be, the decisive act of governing."

The art, or "figures," of the book offer a different interpretation of it at every turn. The dependency of planning on economics and politics (as both power and authority) is revealed by both, what I have called here, the "blank frame" and the "plan." In addition to this significance of the painting, its place in the text violates the "modernist" technical achievement Le Corbusier claims it is. He (1982: 298) states that as a technician he "sought to discover exactly how the development of a city takes place and to find a formula which should give the rules on which modern town planning must rest." However, it ends with this invocation of pre-modern history and the absolutist state. The key feature that would make planning based on rules and formulas achievable—i.e., political authority—is obscured within this rebus at the end and is never discussed. The meaning of the text is not carried off by his skills as a planner, but by his skills of textual strategizing.

3. Questioning the Post-Modern in Architecture and Planning

Le Corbusier's work questions the distinction between modernism and post-modernism in a multitude of ways. I have attempted to analyze many of his textual strategies as ways of undermining that distinction. His attempts to manage a chronology of modernism seem to fail at every turn. Moreover, two major aspects of his text, which may qualify as post-modern, are thoroughly "modern." His creation of a revelatory collage, which invites comparison with the visual culture of post-modernism, is a means to represent the politics of urban development that aesthetics and planning often fail to comprehend. Le Corbusier's use of collage is as much in keeping with the goals set for its use by the Surrealists as it is with that of visual artists now. Furthermore, his text could be interpreted as a prescient description of "post-industrial," often equated with post-modern, redevelopment of cities such as New York, Houston, Los Angeles, Hong Kong, and Tokyo. Yet, what passes for the post-industrial, in cities as well as in texts, may be just as much a manifestation of "modern" industrial capitalist economies. I will examine both of these problems briefly in this section.

First, Le Corbusier's use of many kinds of images points to the actions of demolition, conservation, and construction that are the theory and practice of architecture and planning. This demolition, conservation, and rebuilding are also the methods of collage and montage. Lynch (1961: 19-36) traces the history of the creation of collages to the work of Picasso, Braque, Grosz, and Schwitters between 1912 and 1919. Schwitters used the word "merz" cut from the word, "Kommerzial," as it appeared in a newspaper to describe his early work. Peter Bürger (1984: 78-79) argues that attention to the principle of construction, and not the content, defines "avant-garde" montage in literature, cinema, and painting from 1912 through the 1930's. He writes that what is "decisive are not the events [of works of art] in their distinctiveness but the construction principle that underlies the sequence of events. . . . The recipient's attention no longer turns to a meaning of the work, but to the principle of construction." This is analogous to the tension within the actions of architects and planners. That is the use of the artifacts of the city to create meaning or value, or to merely demonstrate the principle of demolition and redevelopment. But the historical material is less relevant here than the textual material.

In an odd and unexpected way, Le Corbusier's use of montage points to the expanding place of Chinese markets and Japanese capital in the past and future of the international economy of cities. Ivanov (1985: 226) writes of the origins of montage in Eisenstein's films: "The first decades of our century were characterized by the exclusive attention paid to the syntax of various signs, both in art (Cubism, Dada, montage, cinematography) and science (descriptive linguistics, logical syntax, etc.). In this sense, Eisenstein's early films, with their emphasis on montage, as well as his accompanying theoretical declarations, answered the spirit of the times." The connection between montage and Chinese hieroglyphs is more important here. Ivanov draws his argument toward the connection between the problem of the sign presented by iconographic language and montage. Both require close scrutiny of visual signs. The hieroglyph's relationship to montage points to two issues in inquiries about modernism: the concept/metaphor of "writing in general" and the appearance of vaguely Japanese or Chinese characters, which may have no meaning in those languages, as symbols for an imagined future techno-economy in Asia. These may appear in popular culture as symbols for an economy that is more "advanced" than that of the old imperialist West.

The most important philosophical connection of Le Corbusier's work and montage is with the work of André Breton. The Surrealist Movement existed to oppose work like that of Le Corbusier. Breton (1969: 261) wrote in 1935 that Le Corbusier's design of the Swiss Pavillion at the Cité Universitaire at Paris "outwardly answers all the conditions of rationality and coldness that anyone could want in recent years." In contrast, Breton advocated that the "systematic derangement of all the senses" was the purpose of Surrealist art. Breton (1969: 263) writes that he believes,

> in the possibility and the greatest interest of the experiment that consists of incorporating objects, ordinary or not, within a poem, or more exactly of composing a poem in which visual elements take their place between the words without ever duplicating them. It seems to me that the reader-spectator may receive a quite novel sensation, one that is exceptionally disturbing and complex, as a result of the play of words with these elements, namable or not.

With or without Breton's support, Le Corbusier certainly achieved this with his work before 1930. However, one's ability to associate this design for literature with either modernism or post-modernism confounds the very distinction. With regard to the design of cities, that distinction is even more problematic. What Breton hoped to accomplish by the design of literature is accomplished in cities by the near absence of design and planning. The private sector, as it distributes itself among land parcels and buildings, achieves this disturbing sensation with a cunning illogic.

My discussion of politics and planning as well as modernism and post-modernism involves the following discussion of urban economics for three reasons. First, the discursive and physical evidence used to differentiate "modern" from "post-modern" periods represent political and economic changes in cities. Second, Le Corbusier's discussion of the financing of the Voisin Plan for Paris is like much of the discussion that now surrounds discussion of the revitalization of "post-industrial" cities. He leaves unexamined the theoretical and practical ways in which the availability of credit and the power of the private sector to locate according to its plans undermine the ability of planners to "scientifically" plan cities—then or now. Third, the attempt to differentiate philosophical periods depends on a hidden economism; that is, the cause of this "transformation" is often taken to be an underlying change in the relationships between economics, technology, and politics. We can no longer comprehend those relationships through empirical or historical investigation. That investigation requires interpretation of the textual strategies of economic analysis as well. Critics of "post-modern" literature and art leave uncriticized the representation of the "post-industrial" economy itself.

There are many critics who accept the ideas linking the construction of post-modern works of literature and art with the economies of contemporary cities. Davis (1985), Dear (1986), Jameson (1983), Jencks (1984), Perloff (1980), and many other writers assume that there is something about the relationship between cities and the world economy that defines the economic base of post-modernism. Many of the arguments begin from the assumption that there has been a radical "transformation" away from a capitalist world economy or, more specifically, an industrial capitalist economy.

Many of those authors cite Daniel Bell's *The Coming of Post-Industrial Society* as the verification of that trend. For example, Perloff (1980: 15) states, "Cities and metropolitan regions are in the forefront of a major transformation that scholars have variously labeled post-industrial society, the services age, or the communications age." "Transformation" is a metaphor implying substitution and replacement without remainder or excess; that is, this metaphor implies that there is a total transformation of the organization of the economy without remainder of pre-industrial or industrial forms and without micro-organizations of the economy that might be indicative of future forms. However, the continuing use of the word "transformation" implies an identity among discourse, economic theory, the "revitalization" of cities, and the regionally differentiated creation of surplus value, which has globally changed all at once. A close reading of the metaphors of Bell's analysis uncovers the problems in this identity and, thus, in the periodization of modernism and post-modernism.

Daniel Bell's (1973: xvi) initial simile on the economic developments pointing to some new world economy is telling. He compares the "old" and the "new" economies to "palimpsests." The palimpsest is a re-writing; a writing over existing writing or over-writing that which has been erased. The apparent change leaves the initial impression of marks behind. Those initial "traces" (a word of complex meanings for Derrida) can be read through the second writing. That is, the old and the new economy have the relationship of a writing apparatus.

Derrida (1978b) describes in detail, in "Freud and the Scene of Writing," Freud's search for a precise "metaphor" for memory and the meanings, which are "impressed" upon the unconscious. Freud finally uses the device of the "magic slate." Derrida's analysis proceeds through an interpretation of the variety of writing apparati Freud discusses. All are more complex than the palimpsest. The "magic writing pad" consists of a wax layer that retains the initial impression, and another top layer that always retains its smoothness. The writing pad gives the illusion of total change and totally new writing. Yet the layers of overlapping, crossed-out, and partially obliterated impressions remain. The top layer makes a perpetually available innocence; the wax layer maintains an infinite reserve of traces. According to Freud's topography, the work of memory is like the work of the "magic writing pad." What is remembered, however, is subject to "censorship," those partially visible (memorable) inscriptions are rendered visible only according to memory's entire work on signifiers and signfieds (a distinction itself undermined by the notions of writing and the unconscious). The structure of the "magic writing pad" confounds the structure of the sign. It makes the determination of signifier and signified reversible. It facilitates the inscription of new material, which can be read in terms of either of the parts of the sign. The layers of the writing pad pile signifiers on top of signifiers. They form the depths (on a material which has no depth) of fragments of traces and erasures.

Bell assumes that the old and the new economies are a function of technology. There are two palimpsestic structures at work in Bell's book: the relationship of technology and capitalism as well as that of the old industrial and the new "post-industrial" economies. Playing with this palimpsest, one could interpret Bell's comment by beginning with the assumption that technology is the signifier in memory, which is now being collected in order to represent the economy, the signified. However, Bell's argument presumes that technology is autonomous from the economy. His argument suggests that "technology" is inscribing another "economy." Many other arguments suggest that the reverse is actually the case. This is an old debate, of course.

The official inscription of economic discourses and the economy being inscribed creates a memory of our time. The very cuts made by the textual strategies in economic discourses retrace the memory of the old economy. Given the structure of the palimpsest, it is possible to reverse, and deconstruct, the values imputed to the old and new economy. For instance, if we were to use world systems theory or Marxian political economy for readings of urban economies, two readings would be possible. They would also reverse the descriptions of the old and the new economy. On one reading, the old economic base of national capitalist economies, which is the mythical foundation of "modernism," can be seen as dependent on technological change, the international "development of underdevelopment" (Frank, 1969), and the historical changes in a capitalist international division of labor which has existed for centuries.[5] On the other hand, the "post-industrial" economy, which is the mythical economic base of "post-modernism," can be explained (Sassen-Koob 1985) in terms of capital mobility and labor migration. The first rewriting of political economy gives it an international scope and emphasizes the economic structure of colonialism and changing technology. The second is a rewriting of theories relying on notions of a global transformation of the economy though technology. That so-called transformation is then explained by the ability and consequences of capital and labor leaving regions at different times and in different directions. That explanation has much in common with Marx's notion of the "overcoming of space by time." Using that interpretation, we could say that what we see as gentrification, changes in manufacturing and service jobs, increasing class inequality, and the split between new "post-modern" architectural environments and declining neighborhoods is the result of the mobility of capital and not of the disappearance of capitalism.

Gayatri Spivak (1985) has shown how this supposed distinction between the old and the new economy depends on continuist readings of the relationship between capitalism and technology. For my purposes, I will only mention two points from her argument. First, commenting on the business press, she writes (1985: 88-89),

The entire economic text would not be what it is if it could not write itself as a palimpsest upon another text where a woman in Sri Lanka has to work 2,287 minutes to buy a t-shirt. The 'post-modern' and the 'pre-modern' are inscribed together. . . . Regular periodization should rather be seen in its role within the historical normalization required by the world system of political economy, engaged in the production and realization of Value, the 'post-modern' its latest symptom.

The difference between the old and the new economy depends on more than technology; it depends on the normalization of the appearance of that technology within the international "trans-portation" of capital as it engages all the world in the realization of value. Second, Spivak includes montages of designer names and other clothing labels marked with the place of their manufacture. There are pictures of labels and on those labels are the names, Uruguay, Hong Kong, and Korea, among others. The names of clothing designers or retailers and the names of the places of manufacture go together only in the official memory of the "trans-formation" of the world economy. The economic conditions of those places, which we interpret as spacially and temporally distinct periods of capitalism, are quite as visible in places like Buffalo, NY, southern rural Minnesota, and even in New York City and Los Angeles.

The facts of political economy are caught in the political economy of texts which are designated as "post-modern." Those facts are important, but so are the discursive strategies, which elide them in the name of a supposed indeterminate "transition" into the "communications age." Being careful to scrutinize the structure and motion of those texts or those "facts," we should not be deceived by the momentary stability of capital in the places they name. Detailed analysis of the discursive and physical changes in cities reveals that planning depends on political power and authority, not only because political authority makes it possible to implement plans but because more deeply planning *is* the spatial and temporal location of capital itself.

Spivak's collages could be placed in Le Corbusier's blank frame. They fit for two reasons. First, they symbolize the complexities of economic discourses and practices, which are the conditions of possibility for "post-modern" architecture. Second, her collages and analysis represent the space and time of the substitutions of capital and labor, which defeat

Le Cobusier's and our own "master plans." For these reasons, Le Corbusier's work, paradoxically, signifies the incapacity of the "modernist" program to theorize and plan capitalist cities.

In this essay, I have read Le Corbusier's text in a way that problematizes the issue of "post-modernism" and its relationship to time and space. In contrast with the usual interpretation of his work as that of the quintessential "modernist," I began with an analysis of its "postmodern" features. Again, against the usual characterization of him as the principal exponent of the "rational-comprehensive" approach to planning, I read his work in order to discover ideas about politics and political authority. Le Corbusier's strategy of denial of politics is undermined by his use of the postscript (the painting) which supplements the text and the blank frame. The possibility of inserting a representation of political authority, rather than a comprehensive plan, contravenes Le Corbusier's status as a "modernist." In keeping with a way of reading for "post-modern" features of his text, I have attempted to link it to "modernism" in two ways: by discussing its relationship to surrealist collage and by discussing some problems of constructing in discourse an economic base to which the "post-modern" features of the work can be attached. Through this reading I have attempted to write something about the construction of the conceptual oppositions of politics and planning. That construction, however, is never merely textual, and its political economy never merely material.

This essay is a shorter version of a paper presented at the International Association for Philosophy and Literature conference, Lawrence, KS, 1987 and first published in *Theory, Culture & Society* 6 (1989): 241-261. Reprinted here (with revisions) by permission from Sage Publications.

Notes

1. Attributed to Sant'Elia and Ugo Nebbia, 1914. Banham (1983: 126-130) briefly describes the controversy surrounding the manifesto from which I have taken this passage. Here it serves as an example (almost as a stereotype, a snapshot) of expressions of modern planning.

2. In an earlier version of this paper, I included a long discussion of "framing" and "Enframing" from Heidegger's (1977: 3-35) *The Question Concerning*

Technology. That presentation allowed me to work from the ambiguity of technology as ordering and saving in relation to both high technology and poetry.

3. I would like to thank Gayatri Spivak for suggesting this term which guides the discussion below of the Surrealists.

4. The 1966 edition of *Urbanisme*, the French title of this work, contains an "Appendix" of anatomical drawings. The painting is not the end of the book. *The City of Tomorrow and Its Planning* includes another round of graphic representations of organic and mechanical symbols for Le Corbusier's comprehension of the city.

5. The context and controversy surrounding André Gundar Frank's work is explained in *Development Theory in Transition* by Blomstrom and Hettne (1984). Frank's essay (1982), "Crisis of Ideology and Ideology of Crisis," provides a context for economic trends and development theory in the 1970's.

References

Banham, Reyner. (1983). *Theory and Design in the First Machine Age*. Cambridge, MA: MIT Press.

Bell, Daniel. (1973). *The Coming of Post-Industrial Society*. New York: Basic Books, Inc.

Blomstrom, Magnus and Björn Hettne. (1984). *Development Theory in Transition*. London: Zed Books.

Breton, André. (1969). "Surrealist Situation of the Object." *Manifestos of Surrealism*. Trans. Richard Sever and Helen R. Lane. Ann Arbor, MI: University of Michigan Press.

Bürger, Peter. (1984). *The Theory of the Avant-Garde*. Minneapolis: University of Minnesota Press.

Choay, Françoise. (1969). *The Modern City: Planning in the 19th Century*. New York: George Brazilier.

Davis, Mike. (1985). "Urban Renaissance and the Spirit of Post-Modernism." *New Left Review*, 151: 106-113.

Dear, M. J. (1986). "Post-modernism and Planning." *Space and Society*, 4: 367-384.

Derrida, Jacques. (1978a) *Edmund Husserl's Origin of Geometry: An Introduction*. Trans. John P. Leavey, Jr. Ed. David Allison. London: Nicholas Hays, Ltd.

_____. (1978b). "Freud and the Scene of Writing." *Writing and Difference*. Chicago: The University of Chicago Press.

Frank, André Gundar. (1969). "The Development of Underdevelopment." *Capitalism and Underdevelopment in Latin America*. New York: Monthly Review Press.

_____. (1982). "Crisis of Ideology and Ideology of Crisis." *Dynamics of the Global Crisis*. New York and London: Monthly Review Press.

Heidegger, Martin. (1977). "The Question Concerning Technology." *The Question Concerning Technology and Other Essays*. Ed. and trans. William Lovett. New York: Harper and Row.

Ivanov, Vjaceslav Vsevolodovic. (1985). "Eisenstein's Montage of Hieroglyphic Sign." *On Signs.* Ed. Martin Blonsky. Baltimore: The Johns Hopkins University Press.

Jameson, Fredric. (1983). "Postmodernism and Consumer Society." *The Anti-Aesthetic: Essays in Postmodern Culture.* Ed. Hal Foster. Port Townsend, Washington: Bay Press.

Jencks, Charles. (1984). *The Language of Post-Modern Architecture.* 4th Edition. New York: Rizzoli International Publications, Inc.

Le Corbusier. (1929). *The City of Tomorrow and Its Planning.* New York: Payson and Clarke, Ltd.

_____. (1947). *The City of Tomorrow and Its Planning.* London: Architectural Press.

_____. (1982). *The City of Tomorrow and Its Planning.* Cambridge, MA: MIT Press.

_____ and Pierre Jeanneret. (1946-1970). *Oeuvre Complète.* 6 Vols. Zurich: Editions Dr. H. Girsberger.

Lynch, John. (1961). *How to Make Collages.* New York: The Viking Press.

Lyotard, Jean-Francois. (1984). *The Post-Modern Condition: A Report on Knowledge.* Minneapolis: University of Minnesota Press.

Owens, Craig. (1980). "The Allegorical Impulse: Toward a Theory of Postmodernism, Part 2." *October* 13: 59-80.

Palmer, Richard E. (1979). "The Postmodernity of Heidegger." *Martin Heidegger and the Question of Literature: Toward a Postmodern Literary Hermeneutics.* Bloomington: Indiana University Press.

Perloff, Harvey S. (1980). *Planning and the Post-Industrial City.* Washington, D.C.: Planners Press.

Sassen-Koob, Saskia. (1985). "Capital Mobility and Labor Migration: Their Expression in Core Cities." *Urbanization and the World Economy.* Ed. Michael Timberlake. Orlando, FL: Academic Press. 213-265.

Spivak, Gayatri C. (1985). "Scattered Speculations on the Question of Value." *Diacritics,* 15 (Winter): 73-93.

Ulmer, Gregory. (1981). "The Post-Age." *Diacritics,* 11 (September): 39-56.

_____. (1985). *Applied Grammatology: Post(e)-Pedagogy from Jacques Derrida to Joseph Beuys.* Baltimore and London: The Johns Hopkins University Press.

The Return of

Aesthetics to

City Planning

M. Christine Boyer

**Architecture
Cooper Union**

SIGFRIED GIEDION NOTED in *Space, Time, and Architecture*, that town planning, as he called it, was the last department of architecture to take form in any period. Baroque planning, for example, with its emphasis on ceremonial promenades, central focal points, and axial perspective, remained dominant during the nineteenth century, long after industrialization had radically changed not only everyday life but the structure and surface of the city as well. The same could be said today: city planning lags far behind the architectural and structural changes occurring within our cities: changes such as the gentrification of vast areas of the central city, historic preservation in control of larger and larger fragments of the city, the rise of entertainment zones, or the mallification of downtown shopping streets. There are other changes as well, such as the rise of world-class cities, the service centers of late capitalism which reflect the specific needs and spatial politics of multinational corporations. Many of these cities have simultaneously lost or reduced their industrial base. Another transformation is apparent in the development of the polynucleated metropolitan region, an occurrence that makes obsolete the old center-periphery location theories of urban growth.

What does the theory of city planning have to say about all these changes? There are apparent rumblings in spasmodic fashion that something should happen, that city planning might return to focus on its physical form. Tokyo planners may be taking the lead. If Paris was the capital of the nineteenth century, and New York that of the twentieth century, then Tokyo, they proclaim, as the first high-tech city will be the capital of the twenty-first century. On a man-made island in Tokyo Bay a $12 billion teleport of office buildings, cultural halls, and telecommunication stations is being built. A bridge is under construction from this island to the shore where a self-contained village, River City, is being erected, containing hotels, shopping malls, theaters, and high-rise condominiums for 7,500 people. Another 177 projects are on the drawing boards, most of them to be located in Tokyo Bay. All of this is reminiscent of Kenzo Tange's "Tokyo 1960" city plan in which he foresaw that cities of the 10 million population class were becoming consumption cities, their per capita income already far beyond that which was necessary to satisfy basic needs. These cities were organized by invisible networks of communication, information, and energy channels, and consequently it became the task of architects and planners to provide the visible structure of this information society.

In New York City, the consumption capital of the twentieth century, some architects are beginning to call for at least a reevaluation of the building boom of the last decade and a return to ethics that should lie at the core of the profession. Critical of the postmodern void that looms at the heart of the profession, they see a self-serving architecture of gigantic monumentality which is dramatically out of scale with the rest of the city. Representative of corporate egotism and the vapidness of luxury development, the "decotecture" is the result of the municipal government's promotion of real estate development what ever the cost might be to the social and physical fabric of the city. Nobody within the government or architectural profession, much less among city planners, asks what kind of city do we want and why? Recently, *The New Yorker* announced the resuscitation of Lewis Mumford's old column "Sky Line, "which he wrote for some thirty-odd years, because it is believed that New York City is currently in a much more perilous condition than it was in 1931. The city government has been giving the city away: through zoning bonuses to real estate developers that do not deserve or need them; by a passive city planning commission whose infrequent actions tend ignorantly to promote development in the wrong parts of town; by a one-sided development game in which the tax-base is always the winner and light, air, circulation, and the pedestrian, the continual losers. In short, neither the profession of architecture nor that of city planning has any concept or theory to deal with the city as an entity, rather than fragmented into bits and pieces; and neither hold out any vision of what the city might be as it enters the last decade of the twentieth century.

1. Exploiting the Past

In order to determine just how we arrived at this dilemma, let us turn briefly to the basic intention of city planning when it developed during the end of the nineteenth century as one of the disciplinary discourses that spread their controlling forces horizontally across society. City planning's aim has always been to reduce the chaos of city development, to make it a functional whole through:
- Better distribution of land-uses and control over the location of nuisance-uses;
- Regulation of housing conditions for the lower one-third;
- Concern over congestion of people, traffic, buildings;
- A need to improve circulation whether it be automobiles, air, water, sewage; and
- Concern with ceremonial embellishment.

Across the twentieth century, these disciplinary concerns flourished, and as they did city planning became increasingly more abstract, concerned with process and function, while its focus on physical form withered and died. If we trace the development of rational decision-making processes embedded within the theory of planning, we see its level of abstraction advancing from simply means-ends analyses in which there are many means and routes to the one and only ideal master, or comprehensive, plan; to the 1930's strategic choice mechanisms in which it was recognized that there are many routes and many ends, and that choices along the decision route determined what ends could or could not be achieved. Hence planners began to focus on how to guide these decisions, questioning how to obtain the necessary information about urban dynamics in order to develop early warning strategies, and relocating the advisory commission inside government as mayoral and federal advisors. At this point its primary focus on physical city form began to disintegrate and dissimulate.

By the 1960's, with the advent of computers and data banks, city planners began to develop simulation models of urban development; most often related to transportation models based on location theories, which minimized the journey to work, or models of the real estate market used to predict which neighborhoods would likely decline and which would develop according to various public strategies, subsidies, and regulatory interventions. Now it appeared that city development was being guided by automatic decision-making machines, regulated by information flow, feedback loops, context dependent variables and strategies.

If I were going to extrapolate on past trends and talk about the theory of city planning now and in the future, I would say that the fourth level of rationalization which occurred in the 1970's and 1980's following the desire of planners for greater scientism was a mimicking of the algorithms belonging to recursive function theory. Here we see a new concern with pattern languages developing in which a given set of rules generates an ever-changing structure, a circular process in which a series is generated by rules starting from an initial state, a condition wherein each element of the series is affected only by its adjacent elements.

2. Elements and City Form

The point in recursion is to focus on the elements and their series. Certainly this is the case with out post-modern cities—fragmented elements of the city whole are planned or redeveloped as autonomous elements, with little relationship to the whole and with direct concern only for adjacent elements. Fragments of the city are regulated, for example, by special district or contextual zoning, or historic preservation controls, but say nothing about the city as a whole. In New York City, these generative rules are legion: a special district controls the recycling of Union Square as a luxury enclave; new contextual zoning is abetting the development of the Upper West Side in a regenerated 1930's Art Deco format; while great parts of Manhattan stand cordoned off behind the boundaries of historic districts as large as Greenwich Village and the Upper East Side.

To play on the analogy further, this recursive mentality is serial. Mass production is serial so that it is not surprising to find the mass production of city spaces in late capitalism taking on a serial appearance, producing from already known patterns or molds of places almost identical in ambience from city to city: New York's South Street Seaport, Boston's

Qunicy Market, Baltimore's Harbor Place, Savannah's Riverfront, San Antonio's River Walk, the Pueblo of Los Angeles, San Francisco's Fisherman's Wharf, Seattle's Pioneer Square, and so forth.

A pattern language is ornamental. Consumption is the economic role of many of our center cities today, consequently they are becoming places of entertainment, of pure play. As a good percentage of their industrial base has vanished, lessening the need for large working-class populations. Luxury neighborhoods food shops, boutiques, entertainment zones, and television and information nodes are commanding more and more territory and displacing many of the city's former residents, functions, and services. Further pleasurable experience lies in manipulating already known and familiar patterns, hence our urban vocabulary is filled with reiterations, rehabilitations, recyclings, and revitalizations all based on the regeneration of already known symbolic codes. Even our nostalgia for the vernacular could be called ornamental; habitats, decor, eating habits, craftsmanship, were re-valued at the very moment when television culture, agribusiness, and mass consumption invaded the countryside and virtually destroyed its regional identification and material culture.

A pattern language is formalistic. Ornamentation implies the manipulation of pure form, and we have learned increasingly in the last two decades to look at our cities, their buildings and neighborhoods, as aesthetic objects. We have been taught to do so by reading architectural criticism in our newspapers, by studying architectural guidebooks to our cities' hidden pleasures, by following real estate developments, by listening to the outrages of historic preservationists. Whatever the means, we have returned to focus on the aesthetic or physical form of our cities even though this gaze is from a distance; it neither sees the displacement of uses and people, the rapid gentrification of whole areas of the city spreading out from the center's core, nor does it understand the hidden class structure implicit in the development of these formalistic tastes.

Recursion is also solipsistic. Circling back upon itself the recursive mentality fails to develop a critical oppositional stance to the postmodern city. We have developed a *blasé* attitude about gazing at this city. It is after all just entertainment; we are only there to look and to buy. The city has become a place of escape, a wonderland that evades reality, for there is nothing more to think about in pure entertainment. There is no outside world, no place from which we feel alienated, for this formalistic city is known and comfortable; it is above all a place to enjoy oneself. The pleasure is affirmative and far from oppositional and negative.

3. Ruins of Instrumental Action

Something happened in the shift of rationalism from the 1960's simulation models to the 1970's recursion theories. I consider New York City to be emblematic of what has occurred in many other American cities. In 1969, the City published a master plan and an accompanying apology explaining that it was impossible to plan comprehensively for the whole city. There can be no master in control of all her surveys, no scientific rational efficiency expert able to order the city to follow his dictates; this would be undemocratic, an imposition of power projected downward from the top of the city's authority to its people below. Instead, planning must be participatory and democratic, and dictates must bubble up from the boroughs and even lower from its communities. Consequently, city planning became fragmented, decentralized to the boroughs, while communities were given at least advisory control over land-use development and regulation. The idea of guiding the city's overall development so that an equitable and quality environment resulted—this ideal that people could rationally control the future, that society was evolving progressively toward higher levels of civilization, that rational instrumental action always moves from a state of chaos toward that of control, these ideals that stem from the Enlightenment, and which were the very ideals that engendered the profession of city planning in the early 1900's—these ideals were dead.

What I call the crisis of postmodern criticism and the tragedy of city planning is that as a result of our willing acceptance of these lost Enlightenment ideals, we have fallen into a great malaise of relativity in which the legitimation and truthfulness of knowledge, morality, politics and aesthetics are openly questioned. Jean-François Lyotard (1984) has pointed out to us in *The Postmodern Condition: A Report on Knowledge* that the great legitimating metanarratives of modernism are dead. We no longer accept dictates that are handed down to us, nor overriding myths that we must accept without challenge. Instead we want to take part in the discourse establishing what is just or fair; we want to have a say in the process of legitimating society's goals. It appears that planning as an instrument of rational action fell prey to bureaucratic abuse and that we are aware that knowledge and power are intimately linked, not always to our advantage. The most we can expect under such conditions of challenge says, Lyotard, are context-dependent discussions in limited domains of decision making. Lyotard calls language games the narrative knowledge that reflects local needs and directions and enables judgments of legitimacy on performance standards or on how well a set of rules works in limited situations. Truth, for Lyotard, is what works for a given set of rules, in a given language game, at a specific moment in time. Under such constraints, we are asked to abandon any hope for predictive power and to rely simply on strategic power or skill at playing a limited game. Take away a belief in normative values that we all share, and planners simply operate on the standards of their clients—certainly a limited game—or a city merely follows the rules that will generate the most revenue, to the abandonment of any overall equity and progressive concerns.

Michel Foucault (1972), in *The Archaeology of Knowledge and The Discourse on Language*, also has worked against our acceptance of totalizing models of thought, arguing instead for the diversity of generative beginnings, the ruptures of linear historical progression, the dispersion of effects and the incessant rewriting of history and reinterpretation of facts. Totalizing modes of argumentation, he noted, determine what can be said, who has the right to speak, and what will be the logical development of thought. They silence the different, the oppositional, the marginal. All truths are relative—either dependent upon the rules of a limited language game or representational structures that explain things for the moment but will shift with time.

Jürgen Habermas (1983) objects strenuously to all of this relativity: if we abandon the unfinished project of the Enlightenment and reject all legitimacy claims as well as our quest for emancipation from political and economic constraints, then any concept of rational critique or rational discussion disappears. As Habermas notes, all we can rely upon is the claim that something works in a specific situation, regardless of what its lateral or vertical implications might be. We are locked into a mode of unreflective thought, and we fall into nihilistic abandonment of our claims for freedom and moral autonomy. Habermas believes that the legitimation crisis of our postmodern societies lies elsewhere—not in the fall of metanarratives, but in the split of science, morality, and aesthetics into separate autonomous spheres, a position in which each lies unstable and without normative directions. For Habermas, in *Legitimation Crisis* and elsewhere, there must occur a new formulation of reason, which would recognize the claims of each sphere—the scientific, the moral, and the aesthetic—yet provide them with a universal standard of consensus to guide our discourses and justify our actions. There must exist the possibility of appealing to shared values to settle social disputes. Habermas claims that legitimacy rests upon emancipatory communications; in a democratic society we all share the responsibility to challenge, to question, to debate, in order to be able to accept reasonable justifications and reject invalid claims.

We have cycled back to Lyotard's position: Habermas's belief in emancipation, in human freedom, and in moral autonomy are metanarratives, *a priori* normative structures that we can no longer accept as legitimate. Where today can we find a democratically arrived at consensus? The strategic power that is embedded in limited language games rejects the concept of overriding principles or supremative norms. There can no longer be a resort to metanarratives in which emancipation is discursively attained. So what can we do? It seems that the relativity of specific language games, and their rules which apply to limited decision contexts, is in the end conservative and not very helpful in social decision making. On the other hand, any appeal to undistorted communication and universal consensus formation appears utopian and basically not achievable. Somewhere in between there must be a return to the discourse of reasons in which we ask the following questions: Why should we plan our cities? What vision of the future do we hold? What alternatives do we have to guide our actions? We must return to some normative guidelines because we choose to do so, not because a metaphysical other claims these are correct.

4. Return of the Aesthetic

Secondly, in the shift of rationality from simulation models to recursive function theory, we have witnessed the return of the aesthetic to the theory of city planning—a coming forward again of the physical or representational forms of the city. With the relativity of artistic postmodernism generally accepting Lyotard's stance, the aesthetic returns but it does so in a new manner, in a free play of all styles, with a general quoting, appropriating, recycling of images which easily slide over surface structures. The "post-" of postmodernism implies that the aesthetic may return to the same place within planning theory that it once held, but its form and relationship to the city will be different. The question to address in the beginning is why the return of the aesthetic? Simplistically answered, we will find it to be what Theodor Adorno referred to as the long march of the commodity through culture; eventually even city space and architectural forms become consumer items or packaged environments that support and promote the circulation of goods.

Henri Lefebvre, in *La Production de l'Espace* and *Une Pensée Devenue Monde*, has pointed out that in the last half of the twentieth century, we have turned our attention to the production of space, in particular to its formal or designed aspects. Space enters into the capitalist mode of production as both a source of wealth and as a commodity to be sold; it also determines a set of physical and social relationships. Under late capitalism, space reflecting property relations becomes a system increasingly homogenized at the global level yet fragmented and hierarchicalized at the local level. A monotonous and repetitive series of designed spaces— airports, highways, high-rise cities, and spread cities—astonishingly repeated around the world reduce the qualities of regional place to a homogeneous continuum. In addition the optical-geometric allure that surrounds this space creates a gigantic spectacle. These global spaces are filled with all kinds of objects to buy, engendering through these repetitive acts of consumption yet another level of homogenization and boredom. Transversed by satellites, radars, and computer networks, this global space is tied directly back to information centers of the state, so that information itself becomes one more agent of homogenization. While there may still exist some resistance somewhere on the periphery of this surveillance system, it scarcely aggravates the center's control. At the local level, this projected homogenization appears paradoxically to be divided into many distinct fragments: a workplace, a residence, leisure spots, corridors of passage, and consumption spaces. Quantified, measured, and marketed like money or cells, these spaces become marketable and politically controllable. In addition, this fragmented space is hierarchicalized into high/low ensembles—luxury areas, middle-class residential neighborhoods, historic centers, profitable areas—which then are juxtaposed against the abandoned areas of the city, its slums, immigrant districts, and poorer sections.

Many Europeans respond to this global homogenization by looking at America as an early warning system, a vanishing point announcing changes that will eventually affect other parts of the world. They fear homogenization may become pervasive, even erasing our sense of place, history, and memory. In America, Jean Baudrillard (1986) has written in *Amerique*, culture has become space, speed, cinema, and technology. Space is a spectacle just like the streets of New York, which are always vital, moving, cinematic, and televisual, and which become the image of the city itself; or in the Los Angeles freeway, the space of permanent circulation, twenty-four hours by twenty-four hours, which is a ceremony of flux responding to the pleasures of circulating, crossing the city, untying its space without disturbing its character. Thus the fantastic space of the horizontal postmodern city is really its transurbanistic freeways. It is speed that has erased the fragmentation and hierarchies of space and time, homogenized everything to the absolute present. To roll on, to travel, erases our memory, for the world becomes an excess of things, places, and characters once transversed they can be forgotten.

Several urban observers have noted a shift in spatial organization in the last decade or so, perhaps not so dramatically as Baudrillard, but they have observed a rise of what they have called "command and control centers" or "world-class cities." These are the coordination centers for multinational corporations whose activity stretches around the globe. As they have grown, so have their need for managerial services and financial or telecommunication support. In turn these command centers have engendered massive real estate development; new office, retail, residential, and leisure spaces have been produced on their behalf. In their wake have followed residential gentrification, the rise of luxury shopping areas, specialty food stores, restaurants, theatres, and entertainment zones. These command centers may appear homogenous, but their space is actually fragmented and hierarchicalized. Immigrant communities and residential areas of low-skilled service workers have simultaneously grown as the command centers have created employment expansion in the electronics, construction, garment, and food processing industries. Fragmentation is abetted by the rise of yet another spatial rearrangement; instead of being highly centralized or concentric cities, with a core juxtaposed against the periphery, these control centers tend to be polynucleated cities. Integrated by a vast metropolitan-wide system of highways, new business centers with their own entertainment and residential components now find it possible to locate along the linear transportation corridors near the luxury suburban residential areas. In consequence, these cities are becoming increasingly segregated, with sections devoted to luxury and middle classes which have no contact with the poorer, often under-and unemployed classes.

What planning controls do we have to reflect and to channel these changes? Our land-use controls are predominately negative and able to deal only with fragments. The latter, such as zoning and contextual design guidelines, can guide development but only on a project-by-project basis and not when several projects together have an impact on a given area; while the state with its former urban agenda has retreated from its 1960's policies, which ranged from social welfare reforms to housing programs, taking back most of the victories won by the poor. By and large the private market is left in control of the center of these command and control cities, areas becoming increasingly focused on consumption in the 1970's and 1980's.

To every economic formation or structure there relates a cultural form or an aesthetic. The laissez-faire market economy of the nineteenth century only began to see art produced for the market. No longer protected or sponsored by aristocratic or sovereign patrons, artists began to reveal the pain of their marginalized positions, yet they had no other choice than to participate in the new market economy. Their liberated art was at once both critical of and compromised by the popular taste of the new bourgeoisie with its love of show, its tendency toward self-aggrandizement, conformity, and mediocrity, its delight in pure entertainment and fashionable styles. Drawing a distinction between high art and popular culture, the invasion of the market economy was seen as a debasement of pure authentic forms calling for an act of defiance or a stance of autonomy against the impregnation of the commodity in culture. Artists no longer held a position outside of the market economy from which to resist. The spectacle of the nineteenth-century city, witnessed in the displays of new building types for hotels, railway stations, banks, and insurance offices as well as the architectural shows of the industrial expositions revealed how thoroughly the commodity and art had intertwined in the fieled of leisure and company or corporate identification; while the layers of plush velvet and overstuffed furniture, the profusion of exotic interior styles, made it ever apparent that this show of consumer objects spread an insatiable desire for novelty and a taste for the exotic.

It was sometime in the nineteenth century that artists began to produce for the market. The number of such productions, mostly unique objects, remained limited while the developing mass society demanded more and more artifacts and cultural events. Making a lot of money meant saturating this market demand, so an economy of serial repetition arose. A record of a live music concert, a photograph of a painting, or a reproduction of designed household furniture was essentially a copy produced by a mold, the latter used over and over again until it created a stockpile of artifacts. Not all the money earned amounted to pure profit, some of this capital had to be used in the creation of consumer demand to absorb this excess of goods. Consequently advertising developed, along with the management and normalization of standards of taste; in short, attention and money were spent on the production of consumers and the administrative control of art.

Bureaucratic corporate capitalism of the early twentieth century spawned its own form of modernist aesthetic, for now the state became the center of focus, and rationalized or administrated art became a new fear. The invasion of art by politics, by governmental bureaucracies, was a new threat for, it was believed, only a compromised art could result— an art that no longer revealed the traces and shadows of its alienation, that no longer resisted the commodification of culture. Popular culture in its accessibility to the masses, Theodor Adorno proclaimed in *Aesthetics and Politics*, was the social bad conscience of autonomous art. High art must remain aloof and exclusive if it was to be critical and oppositional. "Both [high and low art] bear the stigmata of capitalism, both contain elements of change. . . . Both are torn halves of an integral freedom, to which however they do not add up." An art and architecture of abstract formalism would try to create a radical separation from everyday life although it would never be so clear in practice. High art, the other of popular culture, would constantly be inspired by and contaminated with lesser forms: the circus, billboard advertisements, reflected images from shop windows, as well as the machine, the speed of automotive travel, the power of electricity—these were all sources of visual inspiration for the early moderns. Aesthetic reform as preached at the Bauhaus was expected to result in new social relations, to totally redesign everyday environments from teapots to prefabricated housing, utilizing the latest industrial products and maximizing organizational efficiency; it was expected to liberate society from wants and inequities. But it would be the purities, whiteness, and authority of high modernism, the Cartesian city plan with its static and progressive formalism, that eventually prevailed. The architecture and morphology of the city was as coolly analyzed as the abstractions of geometry and reassembled in rational forms as precise and clear as crystal.

In time, the oppositional and unassimiliated nature of modern art and architecture became canonized: in the museums of modern art, in the advertising images of modern life-styles, in the design of everyday objects and habitats, in the city plans of redevelopment. The actual aestheticization of everyday life that the modernist doctrine proclaimed, the total theatricalization of its environment and its forms of visual communication, in the end produced one more style propelling the march of the commodity through culture. The line supposedly separating high art from popular culture was renegotiated as mass production rapidly consumed endless supplies of new styles and new aesthetic forms. Totally designed environments now become the normal background for our mode of consumption in the post-industrial city. This renegotiated cultural practice reflects the simultaneous deregulation of the economy, the diminution of the state's investment in the physical form of our cities, and its demolition of all social welfare reforms established during the high watermark of corporate capitalism. It was President Nixon, after all, who proclaimed in the early 1970's that there no longer was an urban crisis, as he began to dismantle the federal programs that had subsidized real estate and redevelopment practices in the post-World War II American city. The state would no longer be the central issue, nor administered art the threat. As the state is subordinated to the imperatives of private production, so the return of an affirmative aesthetic plays a crucial role in an administrated recommodification of our city spaces and private interiors. Now it is the boundless energy, the voracious will of capitalism to devour and control art, knowledge, our bodies, space, time, the cosmos, the universe in endlessly expanding waves that becomes the postmodern issue.

The energy of late capitalism is clearly witnessed in its current exploitation of language, an effort that tries to reduce all information to marketable communications. Consequently, the aesthetic sphere becomes one more language game to manipulate and marketable art reduced to forms that are transmittable, receivable, reproducible with ease. Hence the postmodern aesthetic claims to return to narrative forms, searching for an architectural language that communicates with the public, that manipulates simple combinations and patterns that are part of our collective recall or memory. Marketable art assumes there is a subtext to communication that we all understand, hence the parodies of postmodern art and architecture use aesthetic forms which they claim are drawn from our collective imagination. In many ways this current aesthetic returns to the treasure chest of premodern forms to find styles that are comforting, pleasurable, and sensual to be reproduced, recycled, or reappropriated for a reinvigorated consumer market with the new aesthetic rules. This literal going back to an aesthetic of premodernism is meant to erase the orthodoxies of high modernism, along with its oppositional stance, and to replace it with a postmodern gesture intent on exploiting the semantic potential of *heteroglossia*, the ragbag of collection of historical quotations.

Eventually the totally organized leisure space of the postindustrial city, the pedestrian containment of multi-level shopping malls, even the forced pathways through the city impose an intense boredom upon the spectator. The earliest to raise an objection were the French Situationists in the mid-1960's. As Guy Debord proclaimed in *Society of the Spectacle*, alienation occurred at such a level of abstraction that it became an image. The Situationists, in a movement that culminated in France during the student uprisings of 1968, protested this alienation and the passiveness embodied in these totally commodified spaces. By creating "situations," they wanted to turn the spectacle of capital on its head, to change society by changing everyday expectations and experience, to carry out a rebellion against the commodity. But the city of consumption reveling in its own imagery and display blocked any awareness of a reality that might differ from this spectacle of pure forms. A whole complex of looking was held in place by the force of pure entertainment, by the very act of showing, which kept the gaze focused on surface appearances. The return of the aesthetic occurs within this bracketed spaced, as a wished-for return to the city of performance, theater and play. Shop windows, packaged goods, billboards, architecture, traffic, television monitors, and Muzak come to the same focal point—the theatricalized city of spectacle. The Hollywood movie and Madison Avenue advertising of the 1940's and 1950's had taught us to bask in the richness of objects; we were charmed by the rhetoric of their sumptuous and progressive allure. Not surprisingly, the spectacle then turned its charm upon other parts of society: the mass media, the city, art, science, and religion all became entertaining shows and dazzling displays of objects—the materialism we see repetitively confirmed in our postmodern age.

In the 1970's and 1980's, the long march of the commodity through culture crossed over with the flow of capital returning to the centers of the city primarily as real estate investment. In this new mixture, capital turned to the creation of specially designed environments or spectacles intended to lure the new professional classes to consume. The aesthetic as image, representing fashionable tastes, became indispensable to the economy of serial repetition. Museums became totalized environments selling culture through their shops, restaurants, condominiums, and gigantic extravaganzas. The recycling of old market areas of the city, waterfronts and river fronts, main streets, frontier towns, whatever historic mold could be found—these became the background environments or containers for new shopping malls and food-oriented entertainment zones. These culture markets produced secondary effects as well. The new professional classes expected to be entertained while they shopped, so that more and more money was diverted to the decoration of faddish boutiques, luxurious restaurant interiors, refurbished department stores, phantasmagoric hotel, theater, shopping containers until the city took on the appearance of the gigantic spectacle. This aestheticization of everyday life, the spreading out of designed environments, had another effect as well: the further fragmentation and hierarchicalization of urban space into luxury and non-luxury areas. High culture, Pierre Bourdieu has explained in *Distinction*, with its attending purities and refinements, is used by the upper and middle classes to distance or detach themselves from popular tastes and from the realm of economic necessity. "Taste," he wrote, "classifies, and it classifies the classifier," Stylized form at base is a legitimation of class distinctions. Consequently, we can take the current recycling of inner-city neighborhoods, the rise of designed environment from restaurants to historic structures, the pleasures of sophisticated food taste—in short, the whole realm of aesthetic consumption from town houses to sun-dried tomatoes—as cultural reinforcement of urban spatial structures, those of fragmentation and hierarchicalization at the local level, as well as homogenization at the transurban level.

City planners and architects have become the new promotional agents for this stylization of everyday life. The high/low distinction in spatial areas is everywhere in the city of late capitalism: in Manhattan, it extends from Battery City Park to Televison City on the West Side or the old nineteenth-century entertainment district of Ladies Mile and Union Square, near Fourteenth Street, which is rapidly being recycled and upgraded until it becomes a new luxury zone of boutiques, restaurants, nightclubs, residential lofts, and high-style condominiums protected and abetted by new urban design contextual zoning and historic district legislation. The boundaries between high and low art are never clear, and planners and architects find themselves constantly renegotiating their terrain. Take for a specific example the city spectacle of light. Architects have known for centuries the special fascination with light that spectators have, yet this evanescent art which thrilled the public has usually been thought of as popular taste. Fernand Léger claimed that he often talked with Trotsky during World War I about coloring a whole city for "color set free is indispensable to urban centers." In 1937, Léger proposed that Paris be cleaned and scraped by some 300,000 unemployed workers until it became all white. Then the Eiffel Tower would become a gigantic orchestra conductor, where mounted projectors would diffuse by night many colored lights along the streets, and against the white and receptive façades, played to the accompaniment of the sound of music. But Léger's project was rejected, for the high cult of patinas, of the sentimental ruin, of the taste for the dark and the picturesque, covered his thrilling spectacle of light in dust.

Léger (1973) had quite an eye for the spectacle of the city street, being among the first to pay homage to the art of shop windows as a basic aesthetic form of modern city life; as well as the art of the newspaper tabloid with its sensations of temporal discontinuity and spatial dis-orientation that characterized the urban visual experience. He wrote: "On a main street two men carry gigantic golden letters in a wheelbarrow; the effect is so startling that everyone stops to look at it. There is the origin of the modern performance. . . . The street thought of as one of the fine arts!" Léger's city was full of fragmented symbols, aggressive pulsating machinery, and blaring signals of advertising—a hard, intense, vital city, his visual imagery, borrowing as it did from popular forms, was eventually denied by the purities of high art. More recently we have returned to the spectacle of the street, but in another fashion. The Board of Estimate in New York City has just approved new legislation that will preserve the glitter and visual excitement of Times Square—"The Great White Way." The zoning ordinance will require all buildings in the Times Square area to illuminate a 120 foot span of their lower building wall, preferably with electronic billboards. Originally Times Square signs were the result of intense advertising campaigns—the famous smoking ring from the Camel ad—or theater competition that believed the gaudier the sign and the brighter or flashier the light, the more likely to attract the spectator's eye and improve theater attendance. These light shows were popular art, the spontaneous result of theater aesthetics and advertising mentality, an art that is difficult if not impossible to legislate.

Today in our cities there is a tendency to turn light itself, the most spectacular and ephemeral of the popular arts, into a high art—yet another aspect of the return of the aesthetic. Times Square is one thing, but lighting up our city buildings is quite another. We have long been used to the brilliant effects of light on the Empire State Building, the Chrysler Building, the Metropolitan Life Tower, but suddenly the RCA Building has been turned into a blaze of crystal shimmerings. This spectacle has been quick to capture the developer's eye, and now all the gold that glitters along Park and Fifth Avenues is being illuminated by night. In the middle of a Houston freeway, one Saturday night last April, spectators got out of their cars to watch the skyline of their city suddenly ablaze with light. The composer Jean-Michel Jarré had created an electronic composition accompanied by computer generated lights, lasers, and fireworks that turned eleven down-town skyscrapers into an illuminated stage set to the accompaniment of one's car radio—a truly postmodern event. Clearly, aesthetic boundaries have been renegotiated, and with the return of the aesthetic to city form, the popular spectacular arts of city street, lighting, and fireworks have become normalized events in the aestheticization of our everyday life.

The modernist aesthetic was a critical reforming one. If anything, it believed too naively that social change would follow in the wake of its new visual communication. But modern art was oppositional, a form of resistance, as Adorno saw it, since unresolved social antagonisms, otherwise forgotten, tended to follow its shape like shadows. Critical art could easily break the solipsisms of entertainment, for it continually was moved by the sufferings of external reality. Thus art, that is, Adorno's high art as he describes it in "Culture and Administration," must remain separated from administered art: culture suffers when it is planned—its oppositional stance is dulled and its resistance to society neutralized. In such a weakened position, culture easily becomes useful, pure entertainment to be sold as a commodity. Yet Lyotard is suggesting, in a 1978 issue of *Cultural Criticism*, that this position of purity is finished, that postmodernism has broken down the walls of the museum, the gilded frame that once surrounded high art separating it from reality. Postmodernism involves a deplacing and replacing of art; an effort to get outside what we accept as normal city life, only entertainment, disinterested pleasure and to understand its frame-up and its representational order. He tells us it must be the very plurality of aesthetic forms and the opacity of their discourse that eventually will come to stand against the reduction of every aesthetic form to a marketable communicable commodity. We must once again search in the return of the aesthetic to find a position exterior to the market, outside of this affirmative culture, a site from which we can learn the incommensurability of different aesthetic expressions, to experiment with rules of aesthetic production in order to produce new forms not reducible to the codes of market production. On this new journey we have just begun, and as Giedion noted with respect to the nineteenth century, perhaps city planning will once again be the last department of architecture to take a critical new form.

This essay was originally published in *Society*, 25.4 (1988): 49-56. Reprinted by permission of the author.

References

Adorno, Theodor. (1977). *Aesthetics and Politics*. Trans. Ronald Taylor. Ed. Ernst Bloch et al. London: New Left Books.
———. (1990). "Culture and Administration." In this volume, pp. 27-51.
Baudrillard, Jean. (1986). *Amerique*. Paris: B. Grasset.

Bourdieu, Pierre. (1984). *Distinction: A Social Critique of the Judgment of Taste.* Trans. Richard Nice. London: Routledge & Kegan Paul.

Debord, Guy. (1983). *The Society of the Spectacle.* Detroit: Black & Red.

Gideon, Sigfried. (1967). *Space, Time, and Architecture: The Growth of a New Tradition.* Cambridge, MA: Harvard University Press.

Foucault, Michel. (1972). *The Archaeology of Knowledge and The Discourse on Language.* Trans. A. M. Sheridan Smith. New York: Pantheon.

Habermas, Jürgen. (1983). "Modernity—An Incomplete Project." *The Anti-Aesthetic: Essays in Postmodern Culture.* Ed. Hal Foster. Port Washington, WA: Bay Press.

———. (1975). *Legitimation Crisis.* Trans. Thomas McCarthy. Boston: Beacon Press.

Lefebvre, Henri. (1974). *La Production de l'Espace.* Paris: Editions Anthropos.

———. (1980). *Une Pensée Devenue Monde: Faut-il Abandonner Marx?* Paris: Fayard.

Léger, Fernand. (1973). *Functions of Painting.* Trans. Alexandra Anderson. Ed. Edward F. Fry. New York: Viking Press.

Lyotard, Jean-François. (1984). *The Postmodern Condition: A Report on Knowledge.* Trans. Geoff Bennington and Brian Massumi. Minneapolis: University of Minnesota Press.

(photo by Maria Hall)
The landmark "church over the gas station" in Rosslyn, VA. Is it hetrotopia? Hetero-distopia? Or, is it just another mixed-use development addressing the spiritual and material needs of suburbanite Virginians?

The semi-circular colon-
nade of the Federal
Trade Commission
Building (*left*) is mim-
icked in the design of
the Canadian Embassy
(*below*). Washington is
now a city driven by the
appropriation of symbols
which refer only to other
symbols.

(photos by Robert Merrill and Maria Hall)

Arthur Erikson's design "quotes" or serially reproduces the styles of adjacent buildings and thereby calls these styles into question as the Embassy building refuses its own center in the same way that economic and cultural relations between the United States and Canada marginalize or de-center the Canadian culture and economy (*see* p. viii above). The sharp angularity of the superstructure points directly across Pennsylvania Avenue to the similar angles of I. M. Pei's East Wing of the National Gallery. Surrounding the Canadian Embassy are the National Gallery of Art, the Federal Trade Commission, the United States Court House, the District of Columbia Administration Building, and The National Archives of the United States (*see* pp. 155 and 167 below). Encircled by monuments to Art, the Market, Justice, Administration, and Political History, the Canadian Embassy poses as the monumental center which refuses its own centeredness.

Urban Form and

Urban

Representation

Christian Bergum

Architecture
University of Texas

THE SITUATION TODAY in society and urbanism is one of uncertainty and confusion. Upon first examination there seems to be an absence of a set construct for thinking, representing and building. The French philosopher Michel Foucault (1970) often describes this era as heterotopic, as an age of multiplicity, of numerous separate mini-theories glittering simultaneously upon the landscape. In his book *The Order of Things* (1970: xvii), Foucault argued his case for heterotopia and saw coming the end of representation as it was known to be. Yet beneath all this, it was the student of Foucault who was destined to set forth an underlying logic for representation today. In *Simulations and Simulacra* (1983) by Jean Baudrillard, the underpinning mode is a "third order" of things. The characteristics of cybernetic control, digitality, test/feedback and question/answer form the new operational configuration for the generation of whatever is merely real. The implications for urban form and urban representation are striking.

In recent times much has changed. Within the last few decades not only has our mode of thinking undergone revision but also the products of our hands, the arts, and sculpture, and those of our minds, the media, literature and the sciences. If Baudrillard is correct in his analysis, then we are embarking upon a new era, essentially unlike those that have come before. This heterotopic age will become one of simulations, based on the *epistème* of the code and exploiting indeterminacy. The art of Magritte, the Borges tales, and the media critiques of Marshall McLuhan and Walter Benjamin are brought into focus by the philosophers themselves as exemplars of the changes they perceive in contemporary thought. To this we shall extend the discussion to the artwork of Andy Warhol, the cinema of Woody Allen, the media, the process of political polls in society, and to urban representation as a whole.

1. Poststructuralism / Deconstruction

Against this backdrop, the poststructuralist philosopher Jean Baudrillard paints an unsettling picture of contemporary life. Abstraction today has progressed beyond the *classical* and *modern* systems that Foucault once described in *The Order of Things* (1970: xxii-xxii). According to Baudrillard in his book *Simulations*, "Three orders of appearance, parallel to the mutations of value, have followed one another since the Renaissance; they are *counterfeit, production, and simulation*" (1983: 83). "Counterfeit" was the dominant scheme of the classical period, from the Renaissance to the Industrial Revolution; "production" was the dominant scheme of the industrial era; and "simulation" has become the reigning scheme of the current era. Like Foucault, Baudrillard traces these changes in appearance to mutations of the law of value. However Baudrillard takes it further to a third order of simulacrum. Whereas the first order was based on the natural law of value or utility and the second on the commercial law of value or exchange, the third is based on the *structural* law of value and is controlled by the unique metaphysics of the "code."

For Baudrillard, the creative works produced by mankind "proceeded from a universe of natural laws to a universe of force and tensions of force," followed by today's "universe of structures and binary opposition." After the classical metaphysics of "being and appearance" and after that of modern "energy and determination" comes that of "indeterminacy and the code" (1983: 103). "Cybernetic control, modulation, test/feedback, and question/answer" characterize the "new operational configuration" for the generation of simulacra. The computer becomes not only the tool of scientific inquiry, but also the final storage bank of the research. "Digitality is the new metaphysics, and DNA its origin." In the genetic code lies the "genesis of simulacra" (1983: 103) that we mimic today.

For the sociologist Baudrillard, abstraction is no longer that of the classical "figure, double or mirror." No longer is it a "discourse, referential being or substance." And after Modernism, reality is no longer present in the concept of the force that carries the objects or discourses. No longer is abstraction a result of the movement, zeitgeist, synthesis or understanding that carries the figure and the text in tandem. According to Baudrillard (1983: 2), abstraction today is the generation of models and of a "real without origin or reality: a hyperreal." Thereby the figure is the form that precedes the discourse. The precession of figurative (or linguistic) simulacra engenders the discourse itself. So "modeling and genetic miniaturization" or what Baudrillard calls the hyperreal become the dimensions of this simulation, and the "real" is produced from "matrices, memory banks, and command modules" of the hyperreal. The determinancies of the "classical" natural laws and the "modern" conceptions are replaced by the indeterminacies of the contemporary societal and urban codes.

2. The Ascendancy of Similitude, Seriality, and Difference

According to Foucault, the abstractionists of the early Modern movement juxtaposed shapes, words, and the syntax of lines "without subordination." In *This is Not a Pipe* (1982), he shows how the painter Paul Klee (e.g., *Villa-R*, 1928; *L-Platz*, 1931) juxtaposed images and words to draw attention to the subconscious relation between words and objects. Kandinsky, on the other hand, sought to efface all notions of "resemblance and affirmation" that could posit any "equivalence" between the two (e.g., *Improvision*, 1933). Both approaches, but Kandinsky's in particular, resulted in paintings of unrecognizable characteristics. In so doing, the painters had dismissed the "former equivalence between resemblance and affirmation," and "freed" painting from both. The only hierarchy to understanding the abstract painting was to know the painter's intent in the abstractions depicted, the "subconscious relation" as seen by the painter (e.g., Klee) or, conversely, the "action of painting" characteristic to the painter at that particular moment in time (e.g., Kandinsky). Thus the importance of objects and language as things in themselves was replaced by that of the painter's conception, *zeitgeist*, synthesis or action.

René Magritte, on the other hand, set out on a course different from that of the modernists. According to Foucault, he proceeded by dissociating resemblance from affirmation which is quite unlike Kandinsky's double effacement. Magritte does this by "disrupting their bonds and establishing their inequality," an approach which "brings resemblance into play *without* affirmation" (Foucault 1982: 43-44). It is a play that brings alongside with it that quality which is "closest to discourse," the indefinite continuation of the "similar," seriality without end, purging from this kind of painting any sort of affirmation that would suggest a particular referent or what is resembled.

The Surrealist painters attempted to evoke the *mystère*: that ineffable otherness beneath the surface of the objects of common perception. Magritte's art borrows heavily from the writings of Ludwig Wittgenstein, Ferdinand de Saussure and structural linguistics, and the poetry of Apollinaire. Unlike the abstractionists, these paintings have recognizable objects, or portions of objects, yet at the same time are very mysterious. The genetic structure or integrity of an object is mimetically reproduced, painstakingly photographic, though unhinged from any reference to a singular context. The mysteriousness arises when it is purposely brought into play upon, or in intersection with, numerous other "realities," contexts or objects, the one genetic structure dancing with any number of other genetic structures or codes. Magritte's *L'Explication* (1952) presents upon a table top a bottle, a carrot, and a carrot-bottle (the intersection-object). "What explicates what?" is the question asked and not answered. It can be read (answered) in one direction as easily as another as the similar is played upon the similar.

In the initial stages of the movement, Surrealism still expressed some solidarity with the realism it contested. In Baudrillard's words (1983: 147): "it augmented its intensity by setting it off against the imaginary." But in the more advanced stage, it entered into the realm of the hyperreal, he says, in the sense that it equally effaces the contradiction between the real and the imaginary. For Baudrillard, Magritte's art comes very close to achieving this hyperreal stage, whereas according to Foucault, he does ultimately achieve it by refining the difference between "similitude" and "resemblance."

According to Foucault (1982: 43-54), Magritte "dissociates similitude from resemblance" by bringing the "former into play against the latter."

Resemblance characteristically has a "model" or an "original" object that hierarchizes and structures the onslaught of copies that follow forth, however imperfect they may be. Clearly there remains a primordial object, by which copies are judged accurate. Simulation, on the other hand, hasn't any such original or referential order. Similar things beget other similar things and propagate themselves in a series that has neither beginning nor end, that can be followed in one direction as easily as another. There is no hierarchy (other than the hierarchy of propagation). There does not appear to be any "designedness" to it other than one particular trait of propagation and that is its inexactude and inexactness. These mutant things, these simulacra, propagate themselves from small differences

Figure 1. René Magritte, La Trahison des Images: ceci n'est pas une Pipe (1926)
Courtesy of Los Angeles County Museum of Art with funds provided by
the Mr. and Mrs. William Preston Harrison Collection

The hyperreal pipe of circulatory similitudes: it is not a real pipe that is depicted though it certainly resembles one. Magritte's non-affirmative statement breaks with the referential and affirmative bond of the classical form or representation and posits irreferentiality. That is, the inability to say what refers to what. The statement and the pipe are set in play, each speaking or picturing something that is not seen in the other, such that a multitude of different affirmations can be interpreted, with equal force simultaneously.

among small differences. Unlike resemblance, which bases itself on a referent which it reveals and to which it must return, similitude sets free the simulacrum to circulate as an indefinite and reversible relation of the similar to the similar.

Magritte's painting *Ceci n'est pas une pipe* of 1926 (see Figure 1) exemplifies a third order simulacrum. First, it is nonaffirmative, as Foucault suggests; it is *not* a pipe that you see there (although for all practical purposes it is painstakingly photographic). The text suggests it is not. Second, it is directionless and non-hierarchial, for in a "calligramatic" fashion it reads from text to picture or from picture to text with equal force simultaneously. In this way it effectively effaces the beginning and end-point of its interpretation. Foucault in his book *This Is Not a Pipe* (1982: 19-31) gives no fewer than seven possible "interpretations." The "this is a pipe" silently hidden in mimetic resemblance becomes what he calls the "this is not a pipe" of circulating similitudes.

The merit of similitude over resemblance can be understood in its ability to best capture the epistemological dilemma of our contemporary age. The trappings of resemblance lie in that it inherently must make its singular "assertion," always unchanging and targeted by some referential. Similitude on the other hand, enacts a multitude of different affirmations which "dance together." Whereas resemblance distinguishes or measures itself by some particular reference, the similar presupposes no such beginning point, and develops in a circulating series that can go on *ad infinitum* (cf. Ingram 1987). While resemblance refers to "this" or "that," similitude *defers* to neither "this" or "that."

Consider the paintings of Andy Warhol. What does it mean to paint a field of replicated soup cans, dollar bills, soap boxes, or pop bottles? How did this come to be an accepted form of painting? Jean Baudrillard (1983: 151) points to the work of Warhol as a prime example of the acceptance of the simulacrum for the real, and the final realization of simulation in art. Art can become a "reproducing machine without ceasing to be art," he says, since within this third order to things, the machine itself is only a sign. Production loses its societal finality when the utilitarian law of value (i.e., the production of useful objects) is replaced by the structural law of the code (i.e., the production of signs of increasing wealth and prestige). For Baudrillard, the structural or the digital nature of the code propagates along small differences as in the fluctuations of GNP in a fashion similar to the circulatory similitudes recognized by Foucault.

Baudrillard's description of Warhol's *The 50 Marilyns* parallels Foucault's description of a Magritte painting. Each of the numerous ever so slightly different reproductions of Monroe's face is exact in silhouette, yet within each silhouette is the affirmation of what cannot be seen, that which is hidden. Similitude reveals and propagates the sorts of things that the recognizable objects hide, or the familiar silhouettes prevent: the complexions, purple, pink, negative and autopositive, the oversized lips, and the hyperblonde hair, the long line of small differences. In its multiplicity, the Warhol simulacrum engenders the viewer and sends into oblivion the beginning and the end, the original and the real. By similitudes relayed indefinitely along the length of a series, the image itself loses its original identity, and the name it bears. For Baudrillard, it portrays society's acceptance of a simulacrum or a hyperreality for the real.

In society, as in art, the precession of simulacra engenders the populace. Political polls that earlier were merely classical representations of popular opinion as a *fait accompli*, now proceed to engender the populace by formulating "popular opinion" prior to the voting booth. The polls engender the populace and the populace feeds the polls, and who is to say which has more influence upon the final decision. Instant feedback, question/answer are no longer the modes of disseminating reality, but become hyperrealities without origin and are themselves exchanged for the real. According to Baudrillard (1983: 116), we live by the mode of *referendum* precisely because there is no longer any referential.

3. Media as an Encoded Simulacrum

Simulation has entered into all aspects of society. Every sign, every message (including objects of "functional" use as well as any item of fashion or televised news, poll, or electoral consultation) is presented in the form of question/answer. According to Baudrillard, the entire system of communication has passed from that of syntactically complex language structure to a binary system of question/answer and that of the perpetual test. Tests and referenda are perfect forms of simulation. The answer is prescribed by the way the question is framed: "it is designated in advance." Tests and answers depict the ascendancy of the forms of media that Marshall McLuhan (1964) formerly termed "hot." The referendum has the quality of an ultimatum; the unilateral nature of the question goes beyond that of an interrogation, for it imposes a sense that the cycle is to be suddenly completed. Every message is a verdict. The simulacrum of a distance, or even of a contradiction between two poles, is only tactile, a substitution of the effect of what seems like the real for the real.

Consider the public opinion polls, whether televised, radio broadcasted or printed. The influence they have to sway things today is most remarkable. The polls are used by political, governmental, or private groups as a tool to advance their positions. To do so they must frame the question to their advantage, to design for the answer they desire. Take for example, the public's view on the highly volatile question of abortion. The same "American populace" is being polled over the same issue, yet it contradicts itself on the issue when the question is posed differently. A recent article in the magazine, *Money* (March 1988) showed that when the question is posed, "Are you pro-life?" the majority respond affirmatively. But the same public, when polled "Are you pro-choice?" contradict themselves and form a majority affirmative to this. A significant number cross over, so the power of the framing of the question and the role of the polls in the formulation of public opinion are understood as they proceed and engender the populace which is the subject of media commentary and analysis. The polls engender the populace and the populace feeds the polls. So who can say who has influenced more when the final outcome is cast? The acceptance of the poll is society's acceptance of the hyperreal for the real.

The renovated space of L'Enfant Promenade in S.W. Washington D.C.

"The only existing events are those which have a meaning that goes further than their meaning, which are to some extent produced only to verify a law, a correspondence of forces, a structure of a model. . . . It is possible that not only has history disappeared but that

we must further feed the disappearance of history. That is, everything happens as if we were continuing to fabricate history, when we are only—in accumulating the signs of the soical, the signs of the political, the signs of progress and of change— feeding the end of history." Jean Baudrillard, "The Year 2000 Has Already Happened," *Body Invaders*, eds. A. and M. Kroker, NY: St. Martin's, 1987.

Today the video has supplanted the phonographic album as the new form of musical entertainment, and some even prefer the video to the live performance. Like the camera, the video removes performers from the audience; it allows neither interaction between the two, nor the choice for interaction. Submitted in the form of the medium, all possibilities for interpretation are encoded in the simulacrum. Reality is effaced, and the simulacrum is what becomes the real, or the hyperreal. "Did you hear the concert?" is replaced by "did you *see* the concert?"

Woody Allen's film *The Purple Rose of Cairo* contains another third-order simulacrum. In lieu of the *classical* representation whose actors convey an author's script or the *modern* theatre of Artaud which is alive to the extent that it carries its meaning spontaneously, here we have Woody Allen's depiction of the hyperreal nature of circulatory similitudes. "Which reality is real?" is inscribed in a narrative that moves in one direction of "reality" as easily as the other. Like a Magritte painting where the reality of that which is painted intersects with the reality of the painting itself, an actor upon the screen leaps forth into the audience to interact with a viewer, and then the viewer hops onto the canvas screen. Anyone who sees Allen's film is caught within the laughable state of guessing which reality is the real when circulatory similitudes propagate the multiply as the film unfolds.

4. The Simulacrum and Differences

For Foucault, the media simply depicts the heterotopic nature of society today, and its inability to say which "reality" is the "real." For Baudrillard, this omnipresent media depicts the full acceptance of the hyperreal for the real. While both Foucault and Baudrillard focus their critiques on the "circularity" that they find in the media and this art, the philosopher Jacques Derrida in *Writing and Difference* (1979: 105) turns to the critique of "difference" to note that the propagation of small differences acknowledges that things now "defer to" instead of "refer to." Circularity, in itself, does not go anywhere; it is directionless and static. Difference and deference displace the meanings and move the meaning and express this dislocation.

According to Derrida, to "defer" means much more than Foucault's decalcomania, the "depiction of things not seen, formerly hidden." To "defer" means more than to "differ," to mark an unlikeness. It can also have temporal and spatial implications. To temporally defer is to postpone to another time and is the marking of time. Likewise to spatially defer is to mark a distance, such as to defer from here to somewhere else. Essentially, difference and deference exemplify the acknowledgment of an "otherness," that perhaps before was not seen. The deliberate bringing of things, discourses, or approaches that were previously exterior to the one under consideration typifies the deconstructionist agenda. An early example of this was Foucault's problematic attempt to write about madness, mixing sane writing with insane, in the fashion of a "double discourse" (*Madness and Civilization* 1965). In a similar fashion, Magritte paints the strangest intersections of things on his canvasses: "feet-boats," "bird-leaves," "carrot-bottles" (or "bottle-carrots"?) without hierarchy. For Derrida it is the grafting of the genetic fragment of one text onto the other that one searched for, or enacted, for the purposes of de-constructing the preconceived constructs.

While Foucault or Baudrillard do not give any purpose for the arrival of heterotopia or simulation other than the mutations of the laws of value and the epistemological dilemma they depict, Derrida points to the open-endedness, to the lack of metaphysical (political or theoretical) closure they bring about. Trust in this open-endedness is ethical. Those discourses that beforehand were repressed are hereby grafted onto the mainstream discourses for purposes of deconstructing the one *vis à vis* the presence of the other (Derrida 1979: 82-153). Derrida shares Emanuel Levinas' advocation of an open-ended acknowledgment of others, otherness and its encoding and its propagation within the simulacrum.

5. Urban Design and Indeterminacy

These problems of a value system discussed by Foucault, Baudrillard and Derrida lead to the final attribute characteristic of the designer's process—that is, the attribute of indeterminacy. In his book, *Simulations*, Baudrillard (1983: 83) associated the changes in society and art, like Foucault, with mutations in the law of value. According to Baudrillard, the simulacra constructed by man "proceed from a universe of natural laws to a universe of force and tensions of force," and today to a "universe of structures and binary oppositions." In this sense, the designer today relies upon a value system that is based on indeterminacy and the code. Whereas the classical urban designer relied upon the natural value of objects and of language as signifiers, and the modern on the morality of the *zeitgeitist* determination—that is, the value of utility—the present-day urban designer relies on the structural law of value and the indeterminate and binary structure of the code.

The characteristics of cybernetic control, modulation, test, feedback, and question/answer form the new operational configuration for the generation of urban form. Like art and the media, architecture and urbanism are subjected to the same precession of simulacra that engenders its very production.

> It is the generation by models of a real without origin or reality, a hyperreal. The territory no longer precedes the map, nor survives it. Henceforth, it is the map that precedes the territory—PRECESSION OF SIMULACRA—it is the map that engenders the territory and if we were to revive the fable today [Borges' cartographers], it would be the territory whose shreds are slowly rotting across the map. (Baudrillard 1983)

And as the real becomes its own pure simulacrum, it models its own reality in deference to itself. Since architecture and urbanism today are no longer that of the classical image, double, or mirror, nor that of the modern esprit or functionality, it cannot be measured against some referential being, object or nature, nor *zeitgeist* synthesis or concept of functionality, existentiality, or phenomenology. Since it is the generation of a "reality without origin or reality," a hyperreality that subsists here and there in the precession of simulacra that engendered and formed it, contemporary urban planning can only be measured against the precession of simulacra that formed it. The integrity of the engendering simulacra must be maintained. In a fashion similar to Magritte's, who paid close attention to mimetic detail and to resemblance of the objects he chose to toss into his paintings, the designer must likewise, under the structural law of value, pay close attention and maintain the character of the paintings or objects that have engendered, according to his choice, the final urban realization. In this way, Magritte's paintings evoke that mysteriousness: that ineffable alienness beneath the surface familiarity of the world. Unlike early modern abstractions that often dissected objects

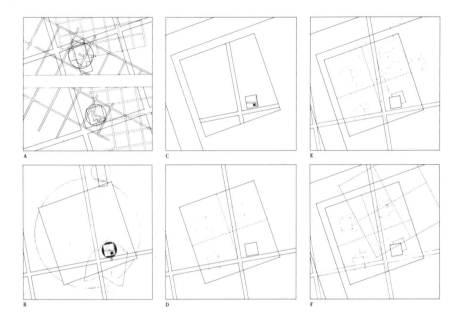

Figure 2. James Tilghman, excerpts from weekly discussions in the Eisenman Studios at Harvard GSD, 1983-1985. Text and drawings reprinted by permission of the author from *Investigations in Architecture*, Jonathan Marvel, ed. pp. 56-57.

Discontinuity is about the presence of absence. It is similar to Freud's mystical writing pad, where you make a mark, lift the page up and the mark is gone, but a trace is visible on the underside. Architecture can be like a mystical writing pad, whereby the traces of former and future conditions exist like a palimpsest.

We are making natural phenomena. In a certain way we are simulating the attitude that the fractal simulates for natural or mathematical phenomena. We are not dealing with either natural or mathematical phenomena, rather we are going to simulate that attitude. The presumption is that if we model our discourse on these parallel discourses, we can discover potentials in architecture to formulate discourses other than the traditional Euclidean mode.

• Recursive means a self-referentiality. It needs its previous and future incarnations in order to understand it.

• It may iterate the attitude of its past and prefigure the attitude of its future, but what it produces will not be the same.

• Self-similarity is a product of this recursive attitude, and self-sameness is a trivial case of self-similarity.

One of the limitations that I perceive in classical architecture is the fact that gravity forces one into orthogonal systems and that anything not in an orthogonal system is seen as expressionistic, romantic and non-rational. I'm not convinced that such is the case. I believe that we can have a rationale, in the sense that there is some systematic attitude outside of an orthogonal condition.

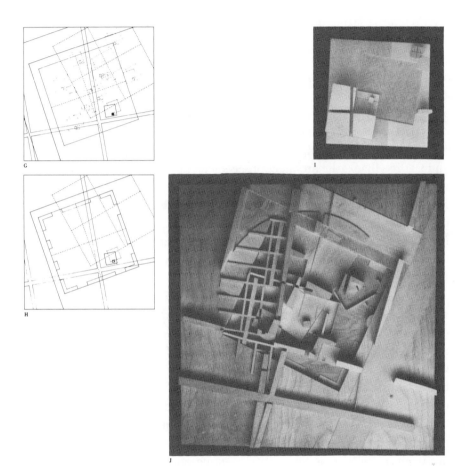

A.- Site contains three scales using the two mounds (circles) as points of registration for the first scaling. Second scaling: State of Ohio, state capital Columbus above, and previous capital Chillicothe, below. Third scaling: Town of Chillicothe; town hall above, and previous town hall below.

B to H.- Different operations occur when "use" is introduced. The use constraint for this project is a town museum for Chillicothe. The museum became a museum of itself, thus its repetitive regeneration in D, E, F and G.

I.- Model of a museum as a "use" constraint.

J.- Model of the museum "in situ" in the town of Chillicothe.

resulting in paintings of unrecognizable objects and characteristics, Magritte's objects are highly discernible, recognizable, and familiar.

So too the urban designer adheres to the character and detail of the objects he has chosen. In this way the Civic Center Master Plan (Escondido, CA) of the architect Eric Moss can be measured as to how well it does or does not carry the spirit of the two-dimensional collage onto three-dimensional form. The model, due to its third-dimension, is wholly of another reality than its two-dimensional partner yet must refer back to it in all its aspects. This means that the collage-essence must be translated to the model in plan and detail. Through the process of question/answer and test/feedback, the architect proceeds to model into three dimensions what was beforehand only in two. Moreover, the dialogue is self-referential by nature, for it always refers back to the originating simulacra. Because the originating simulacra contain circulatory similitudes—in this case collaged portions of plans engendering the idea of an architectural whole— these circulatory similitudes propagate themselves and multiply in the final three-dimensional model.

Consider the various examples of urban design schemes of the recent studios of Peter Eisenman at the Harvard Graduate School of Design (see Figures 2 and 3). The various portions of Columbus, Ohio, and suburb are cut into fragments, rescaled and reassembled into a collaged pattern, with the genetic informants of each juxtaposed one upon the other, at times transparent and overlapping, and at times with striking edge conditions or spliced boundaries. These urban hyperrealities are in themselves a new and indeterminant code, containing multiple "realities" that are insubordinate to a larger whole, glittering simultaneously. They are irreferential and unhierarchial. The certainties of the classical and the modern schemes are replaced by the uncertainties of circulatory similitudes.

These urban representations from the Eisenman Studios are neither abstracted syntheses expressing new visions, nor the recalling of referentials referring to origins and ends. They are the expression of writing, of urban form as *re-writing* and *deference*. In the manner of the archeologist, they excavate from the Ohio landscape and urban grid, without preconceptions, the things that are already there, and, as Derrida would, they graft these genetic fragments, discourses and texts, even if rescaled or realigned, one upon the other. In the fashion of a series, of a Warhol painting, a field of urban representations are arrayed that defer to each other by the act of rescaling, realignment or juxtaposition. Reading in one direction as easily as the other, all possible readings are encoded in advance—origin and end are effaced. Urban scale as it was previously understood is now partially effaced.

Compare Figure 2 with Figure 3, the multi-block urban fabric with the individual street-corner plot. The multiplicity of grafts nearly permits it to be re-read *vice-versa* with equal force—the plot for the multi-block (for example). Surely these forms function and have aesthetic appeal. It could not be satisfactory urban form otherwise. But it is clear that they do not begin with the "use-value" approach of zoned functions brought to form, nor that of the "object-value" system of landmarks interconnected. The city based on the structural law of value is not a *cité industriel* or a City Beautiful but a city-montage. Not an Osaka nor a Washington, D.C. but a Los Angeles, and as such it works and is seductive.

Just as these studio examples efface the reference of scale, likewise they deconstruct "use" and "aesthetic." The city of distinctive mono-zoning gives way to undirected hetero-zoning, just as mono-progammatic buildings themselves give way to hetero-programmatic buildings. Work "here," play "there," and live "elsewhere," gives way to a "work-play," "live-work" and "play-live" heterotopic urban fabric. Although the cottage-industry, recreational-housing, and home-office set-up does not do away with the need for a transportation infrastructure (for it does not do away with either spatial or temporal deference), it does evoke an increasingly heterotopic realignment of such infrastructures, what Eisenman himself calls "decentering use." Jeffrey Kipnis (1985: 45) notes that "Eisenman proposes that contrary to the tradition of architecture, it is not self-evident that origin (in any of its guises: program, history, etc.) 'naturally' governs the design of built environment. The metaphysical status of origin in architecture may be the expression of an unsustainable anthropocentrism."

In the aesthetic sense, these studio projects are complete deconstructions of the referential orders of beauty. They depict a geometry that can be read at multiple levels. The humanistic notion of human-scale reference is unhinged and juxtaposed onto the modernist's motopian scale (e.g., Le Corbusier's buildings that are designed to be seen from speeding down the freeway), or onto movement-scale (e.g., the Futurists, St. Elia), and are grafted without hierarchy. Surfacing from this is another kind

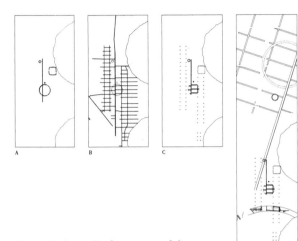

Figure 3. Agus Rusli, excerpted from weekly discussions in the Eisenman Studios at Harvard GSD. Text and drawings reprinted by permission of the author from *Investigations in Architecture*, J. Marvel, ed. pp. 50-51.

Success is probing the limits of discretion. There is no correct way to behave. Failures do not exist in the studio, and we are suspicious of everything that looks like a success. An aesthetic practice takes organizing principles for granted. It does not question them. It does not involve them in its discourse. It assumes them to be fixed and operates on them. Therefore, an aesthetic practice never transcends the aesthetic realm. A critical practice involves both organizing principles and constraints, not as givens but as things that discretion is constantly probing and qualifying.

We are going to deal with the problem of scale which I believe is one constraint. There are three different kinds of scale. One is scale as it relates to a single building or a single unit on a private or unitary scale. It can be called scale specific. A second scale that is also scale specific is public, that is, non-unitary—it refers to things other than itself: its context. A third scale is scale non-specific and self referential. These three scales can be seen as an organizing principle and scale itself can be seen as a constraint.

The second constraint is reading or notation, with the organizing principle as marking. In marking we will deal with presence and absence and with the presence of absence. Another constraint is use as reading. This is where two constraints overlap. That is where reading deals with the nature of the capacity to signal, that is, the capacity to mark. Use is also about the use of signaling as a necessary constraint.

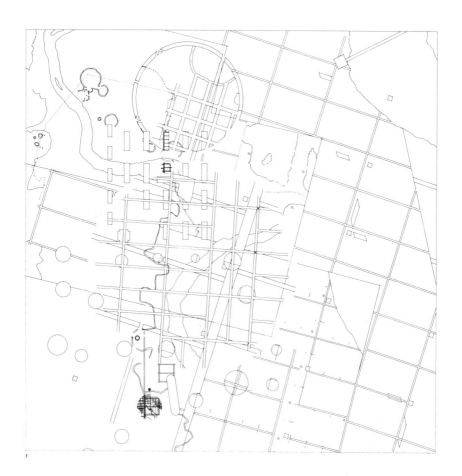

A.- Ancient Indian burial mounds. B.- Resurrected layout of Camp Sherman as it was built over the Indian Mounds. C.- Discourse selects the traces of the Camp Sherman Grid as they intersect with Indian Mounds. D.- First scaling of the previous drawing, using the mound that was never destroyed as a point of registration. E.- Second scaling now introduces the twon of Chillicothe using the library of Camp Sherman (the only currently standing structure from the Camp) as a point of registration. F.- Third scaling introduces the City of Columbus, the current capital of Ohio, using the town of Chillicothe (the former state capital) as a point of registration. G.- Model of the Third scaling.

I have always urged that a column does not just hold up a ceiling; it is also a sign of its capacity to hold up a building. It is actually holding something up, i.e., it has a sign of doing and it could also be a sign of another use, that is, all architectural elements could be both present and absent and could be the sign of another use—the use of the constraint of reading.

of aesthetic order, a third-order aesthetic of not-knowing. Pathgrids are interchanged for roadway-grids, walls for pathways, roofs and enclosures for pavements and terraces. "This" aesthetic and "that" aesthetic are replaced by a hetero-aesthetic and a hypergeometry. It is an unfinished, open-ended and uncompleted aesthetic that defers to ongoing re-reading.

The acceptance of the urban simulacrum has arrived. The political situation today has effaced its origin and its referent in the populace as Baudrillard suggests. In politics and the process of urbanism, it surely has arrived. Today cities and whole regions are increasingly being designed by referenda. The 1988 election in California produced no fewer than thirty-nine statewide referendums and countless county-wide and city-wide ultimatums. The democratic process nearly comes to a halt. Elected governmental officials cease to carry out what was preconceived to be, by fact of their being elected, the will of the people. Rather, the choice is to operate by referenda precisely because there is no longer any such referential.

By the way the referendum poses its questions, it designates in advance the answer. Who wouldn't vote for a "Prop. XYZ" that is anti-traffic congestion? No one is pro-congestion. Yet halted by its enactment, in the City of San Diego, for example, was the construction of housing beyond an 8,000 units per annum, half its normal rate. By May the following year, home builders, architects, planners and planning commissions were out of work; the 8,000 target had been exhausted. By June we read in the local papers that "A New Commercial Boom had Awakened in San Diego." Is this any way to build a city, one planner asks? Who can plan when we live by referenda?

What would a city look like, what would be the character of its urban form after thirty years of design-by-referenda? Would it depict an indeterminate and unhierarchial array of urban fragments, partial texts laid one upon the other? Would it look like the multi-centered Los Angeles or Phoenix: the decentering of the center into a multitude of mini-centers glittering simultaneously across the landscape. Consider the fragmentary or sudden political willfulness of a beforehand repressed group that chooses to self-incorporate into its own small town within a larger town. West Hollywood has a recent example. Out of that referendum, a new small-town center within a larger town center was enacted, and the grafting of a new text onto the former.

While not-knowing in advance what urban form should be, that "this" zoning and not "that" zoning should go, or "this" monument instead of "that," the urban designers of the Eisenman studio grafted one fragmentary text upon the other in a fashion without hierarchy in a way that aptly depicts the indeterminacy of our urban code today—and the possible urban form to come.

Since the iconology of the classical and the determinancy of the modern conception are now replaced by the indeterminacy of the code, urban form no longer has to be rational, for it is no longer measured against some conception or negative instance. Thus, this new form of urbanism is unusually indeterminant, and merits as much consideration as the classical or the modern forms. The joy and wonder of excavating and uncovering new forms is a pleasure not only to the builders but to the public at large. The recent architectural competition for a performing arts complex at the Ohio State University provided fine entries from both the classical (post-modern classical) and the modern, yet the jury chose the one that they probably understood the least—the one that seemed most puzzling with familiar forms engendering one another in a most uncertain fashion and appearing as a whole unsatisfyingly incomplete. The precession of simulacra, in this instance, objects, pathways, streets, and buildings found on site are cast into juxtaposition, each engendering the other, like a Magritte painting or a Libeskind drawing: disturbingly unhierarchical and full of circulatory similitudes. The acceptance of the urban simulacrum or a hyperreality for the real comes in an age when, by means of similitude relayed indefinitely along a series, the image itself along with the idea it carries loses its identity.

Urban form is offered as a pure simulacrum. In this sense, it is indeterminate and irreferential. The public must now exchange their role as "users" and become "readers." It is no longer offered to them as a designed synthesis, but as John Whiteman (1986: 6-13) reflecting on the Eisenman Studios suggests, it is offered as a fragment of "writing" that the public must now decode for themselves. It is not a completed synthesis of forms, but incomplete and highly seductive. The urban simulacra, like the paintings of Magritte or Warhol, the poetry of Apollinaire, and the television media present a multitude of circulatory similitudes neither this nor that, which exhibit in themselves already all the possibilities of interpretation. Rather than there being a singular set of predetermined "readings" or "uses," there are now a multitude of possible "readings" and "uses" that have not yet been named which the public may encode and enact. These urban forms not only survive the onslaught of referenda, they fully engender them. They are, in fact, the representations of them by simulation.

6. Is This Urbanism?

"Is this urbanism or urban form?" you ask. Or is it painting, collage, montage, or something else? Before saying "yes" or "no," it is sufficient to say that it is an urbanism of another sort. This third-order urban form arises from the indeterminacy of the structural law of value rooted in the contemporary dilemma of epistemology.

> The basic argument for this essay was set forth in a paper delivered for the "City of the 21st Century Conference" held in Phoenix, AZ, April, 1988

References

Baudrillard, Jean. (1983). *Simulations*. New York: Semiotext(e).

Derrida, Jacques. (1979). *Writing and Difference*. Chicago: University of Chicago Press.

Eisenman, Peter. (1985). "The End of the Classical." *Montana State Architectural Review*, (Spring): 2-11.

Foucault, Michel. (1970). *The Order of Things*. New York: Vintage Books.

_____. (1982). *This is Not a Pipe*. Berkeley: University of California Press.

Ingram, Catherine. (1987). "Slow Dancing." *Inland Architect*, (Sept.): 37-42.

Kipnis, Jeffrey. (1986). "Star Wars III: The Battle at the Center of the Universe." *Investigations in Architecture: Eisenman Studios at the GSD: 1983-85*. Ed. J. Marvel. Cambridge, MA: Harvard University Graduate School of Design.

McLuhan, Marshall. (1964). *Understanding Media: The Extensions of Man*. New York: McGraw-Hill.

Marvel, Jonathan Jova, ed. (1986). *Investigations in Architecture: Eisenman Studios at the GSD: 1983-85*. Cambridge, MA: Harvard University Graduate School of Design.

Whiteman, John. (1986). "On the Classical Representation of the Human Soul and Its Denial." *Investigations in Architecture: Eisenman Studios at the GSD: 1983-85*. Ed. J. Marvel. Cambridge, MA: Harvard University Graduate School of Design.

Spatial

Narratives and

Political Space

Harris Breslow

Inst. of Communications Research
University of Illinois

Traffic control must take in all the functions of a collective life. The growing intensity of these vital functions, always checked against a reading of statistics, demonstrates the supreme importance of the traffic phenomenon.

Present-day technical facilities, which are constantly growing are the key to town planning. They imply and offer a total transformation of existing legislation; this transformation must run parallel with technical progress. (CIAM 1928: 111)

What has changed is the orientation from the miraculous to the utilitarian. The steam engine . . . combines utilization of the vacuum condenser with transmission of movement; and the machines of the textile industry show the same cunning mind for decomposing and recombining movements that created man-like automatons. . . .

The artists resort to elements such as machines, mechanisms and ready-made articles as some of the few true products of the period, to liberate themselves from the rotten art of the ruling taste (Giedion, 34 and 44).

Introduction: Space = Place/Movement

NO MATTER WHERE one wants to date the beginning of modern architecture,[1] one of the principles that comes to inform the entire discipline starting roughly from the end of the First World War is that of space = place/movement. None of the terms can be seen separately from the others, for it is with the onset of this discourse within modern architecture, and its subsequent domination by an avant-garde[2] that place and movement come to inform simultaneously the concept of architectural space: the institution of the free plan, where interior space becomes as openly flexible and encouraging of movement as possible;[3] conceptions of *La Ville Radieuse*, the moving city, where social harmony and communal space are invested with—and thus subservient to—the principles of traffic and transit as paradigmatic of and synonymous with urban space;[4] the graphics of the Bauhaus, designed to float on the paper, freeing type from the formal conventions of space, size and alignment; Moholy-Nagy's Fotoplastics, literally forcing the viewer's eye to gestalt through several orientations within the work. All modern architecture, as well as the "ancillary" disciplines of graphics and design, becomes an exercise in combining the principles of space=place/movement. Perhaps Sant'Elia and Marinetti (1914) said it best:

> [We] have enriched our sensibility by a 'taste for the light, the practical, *the ephemeral and the swift. . . .*' We must invent and rebuild the *Futurist city*: it must be like an immense, tumultuous, lively, noble work site, dynamic in all its parts; and the *Futurist* house must be like an enormous machine. (35-36, emphasis in original)

This emergent emphasis must be seen as a radical departure from more traditional architectural conceptions of tectonic space. Indeed, I want to argue that modern architecture could not start until the arrival of an avant-garde (Le Corbusier, the Bauhaus, De Stijl, Wright, the Futurists, etc.) which simultaneously espoused a political intent—the introduction of an aesthetics for a new world to accompany the rational order to be established with the end of the war—and an articulation of space that privileges movement. Prior to this gestalt, architectural conceptions of space were conceived in ways that enunciated space and place together in a formula that may be seen as space=place; spatial constructs were given over to ideas of situation and emplacement, or perhaps more accurately, of stasis and arrival. Having travelled from one spot to the next, perhaps having journeyed to a specific office to petition authority or engage in a commercial transaction or to a place such as a city square to meet up with friends, the individual was located in a place which defined his or her having arrived. The act of travelling and arriving is constructed retrospectively to enable one to gain a sense of the narrative of the act, and through this combination of narrative conjunction of arrival+situation, *identity and place* are themselves articulated.

Here, then, (at the emergence of modern architecture) it would seem that there are two spatial articulations on the nature of the individual: one calling for a specific siting of the subject, and implying a specific, synchronically static social order (space=place); the other (space= place/movement) placing the individual within a continuously shifting conception of the social, both diachronically and synchronically, so that anywhere in the social fabric the subject exists within a continuously shifting series of social positions. Sociology has long known the implications (and risks) of the second conception,[5] but rather than risk undermining the discipline it continuously fights a rear-guard action to epistemologically legitimate an essential social fabric.

1. The Social and the Spatial in Deleuze and Guattari

In *A Thousand Plateaus*, Deleuze and Guattari enumerate several functions which the state must carry out in order to secure an enunciated control over specific groups within a specific space and time. The state must create both social and spatial fixities; the former, as strictures, channel activity into areas that are both profitable to the group and predetermined by the form of the enunciative codes of the state itself. The latter channel movement through a series of conduits necessary to bleed off the excess and heterogeneous energy of the social in its day to day activities (Deleuze and Guattari 1987: 361-363).

This double coding by the state, the double enunciation of law and movement, occurs in distinction from what I want to call the "smooth surface of indeterminacy," the idea that that which is uncoded (existing outside of the state's bounds) is unformed and as such heterogeneous, uneven and freely associational. There are two reasons for this distinction: first, the state must create and maintain this distinction in order to define itself as an order; that is to say, it must legitimate itself by asserting the functionality of its functions, against what it automatically posits to be an undifferentiated social space, space that has in some way escaped the influence of the state's coding function. It has to ward off, as it were, conceptions of an undifferentiated field or a field of limitless possibilities— such possibilities being presented as the result of living outside of the restrictions of the state's code—against the state's field of coded necessities or imperatives, which it posits as possibilities or potentials in order to simulate the dynamics of the unencumbered order while maintaining its control. Second, in bringing about the distinction between the coded and the non-coded, the "laminar and the smooth" (1987: 361), the state creates the idea of a homogenous social whole as distinct from non-differentiated social entities and spaces that exist outside of its confines: in so doing it is able to spatially segregate its territory in a manner that is symmetrical to its enunciation of the socius. Consequently it enunciates, however temporally bounded, the identification of the state, the nation, and geographical territory.

2. Le Corbusier's Embodiment of Subjectivity and the Modern State

In his comparison of Le Corbusier's *Villa de Monzie* (Garches) with Palladio's *Villa Malcontenta*, Colin Rowe (1976) has noted that one finds similar volumes and proportional rhythms, and yet Le Corbusier

> obtains a compression for his central bay and thereby transfers interest elsewhere. . . . The one scheme is, therefore, potentially dispersed . . . and the other is concentric and certainly hierarchical. . . . At Garches . . . the exploitation of the structural system . . . places equal interest in both center and extremity. . . . Thus a central focus is stipulated, its development is inhibited; and there then occurs a displacement and a breaking up of exactly what Palladio would have presumed to have been a normative emphasis. (1976: 2-7)

I want to assert that within this series of spatial transference Le Corbusier tectonically describes both the social and spatial coding present in the fullest sense of the modern state. We can take for granted that the modern project has as two of its chief goals the liberation of the individual and the simultaneous emplacement of a state which grounds the radically free self.[6] Le Corbusier's spatial coding articulates these two narrative strings (freedom and unification) within a tension that at first radically centers the subject spatially, in a centering and compressing which emphasizes the consonant whole, but in the next moment releases subjectivity to the extremities of the centrifugality of the spatial's limits—

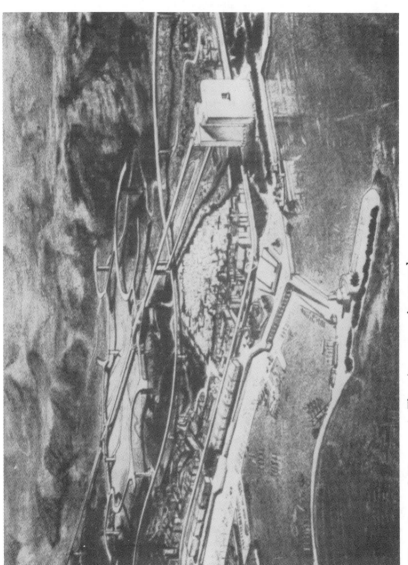

Hierarchy and Movement: The city as transit network. *(photo courtesy of the author)*

the dispersion of attention, the centrifugal aspect of Le Corbusier's free plan, the ultimate freedom of the individual within the constructed socius.

Le Corbusier's plans for traffic networks and high speed transit systems are a perfect continuation of the centrifugality of the *Villa de Monzie*. As noted above, Deleuze and Guattari maintain that in order to reproduce social control, the state must also produce spatial control so that individual and group movements are subordinated

> to conduits, pipes, embankments, which prevent turbulence, which constrain movement to go from one point to another, and space itself to be striated and measured, which makes the fluid [the social] depend on the solid [the striations, the code] and flows proceed by parallel, laminar layers [specific channels of discourse and movement]. (1987: 363)

Le Corbusier's genius lies in the fact that he resolves the tension between the centered and the dispersed sides of modern subjectivity by radically emphasizing the role of the state. This is because he abandons the concepts of the unified self and the centered space, in favor of a radically free being fully controlled by state structures, in his plans for transit nets, for super highways built under the city, for a rigid social hierarchy that informs urban planning and would be linked only through transit functions,[7] Le Corbusier constructs a monstrous vision of the free-plan abstracted to a general social level, setting the individual radically free and in motion while subjecting him or her to an overwhelmingly controlling spatial series which does not so much allow the individual "freedom" as it does perpetuate movement within a tightly prescribed (read socially enunciated) spatial plane.

There are two consequences of this recoding of space. First, Le Corbusier radically calls into question any theoretical stance that informs subjectivity through position, that is, which centers the subject in a diegetic or spatial position. Lyotard's narrative mechanics, for example, relies on the assumption that the progression of social narratives requires a socially static/spatially grounded subject as its linch-pin. The individual is characterized as the central and reciprocating site of an infinite series of intersecting dialogues within the larger social framework (chs. 4-6). Lyotard's narrative mechanics, then, can be historicized within the larger framework of tensions outlined above; if we admit as fact that the transition from space=place to space=place/movement occurs at a point when subjectivity undergoes a reconstitution, it then becomes apparent that what Lyotard is describing is a theory of subjectivity that is more commensurate with Beaux Arts[8] conceptions of space and subjectivity, some of which survive through the modern moment. Lyotard describes a subjectivity which is essentially static and which ignores the modern innovation, namely that subjectivity is in a constant state of flux.

In the modern articulation, the subject can't be understood solely through the site, for both the subject and the site continuously shift. Seen tectonically, the concept of space=place/movement is an asymmetric formula. "Place" and "movement" negate each other given their mutual opposition at an ontological level. The right side of the equation, because of this inherent internal opposition, cannot equate with the left side, "space," thus threatening to nullify the concept of the spatial. Imparting or articulating the idea that space can be neither static nor situating questions the ontology of space itself. Le Corbusier resolves this problem through a reduction in the formula to space=movement as seen through the enunciation of the transit map which, at the general level of the social, abstracts the idea of movement until it is incompatible with the idea of place. Place/movement, once an irreconcilable opposition, as exhibited in the tension found in the *Villa Monzie*, is displaced in a dialectic that creates the reduction to space=movement. Le Corbusier offers an implicit critique of Lyotard because his resolution of this dilemma—which Lyotard sees as a starting point for a mechanics of narrative, thus of ontology—not only dissolves subjectivity (place), it also signals that the concern for a specifically sited subjectivity—a pragmatic which is at the heart of Lyotard's project—was historically quite limited to begin with.[9]

Second, Le Corbusier's fixation with movement indicates a mutation in the mapping of state control over the individual in constant flux. Alongside the idea of the unsited individual, modern architecture develops the notion of movement as the best way to serve the needs of the public which, as a body with needs within some form of mapped space, is always already the creation of the state. Here, then, the articulation of fluid space corresponds not only to a shifting conception of subjectivity, it also signals a new state structure. This new state structure does not rely on the creation of grand institutions or master narratives and with these the creation of fixed and siting spaces; rather it thrives on the concept of transition, the desituation of spatial fixities, and the constant movement—diegetically, ontologically, and spatially—of the members of its population. The representative architectural figure here is Mies van der Rohe, both in his call for the modern building to serve the interests of state and capital bureaucracies,[10] and in his perfection of the curtain wall. The latter represents the grid, the fully enunciated map of the empowered state, as the International Style's paradigmatic global ornament. The grid does not relate to any one nor to any place; it only refers to the emplacement of the map, which, because of the lack of any social or spatial referent, is itself desited. In other words the grid signifies a globally territorialized spatial order precisely because it is not assigned to signify any single place. The International Style, then, is the global generalization, the enunciation on a global scale, of a modern state and capital bureaucratic apparatus which thrives on the movement and speed of its social body.[11]

3. The Reintroduction of Nomadic Space into the State

In *The End of Organized Capitalism*, Scott Lash and John Urry present an analysis of the tension between the growth of state legal structures and the growth of corporate capital structures. Lash and Urry argue that one can see three phases of corporate growth. The first phase, nascent corporate development found in regional corporations, was fully bounded by state legal control. Because of the limitations of the size of the corporate entity, the corporation was an ineffectual actor within the sphere of state politics. The second phase, that of national growth, saw corporations fully expand to the limits of state control, both legally and spatially. The size of corporate economic power had, by this point, caused states to limit the activities of corporations through a series of legal controls that allowed the state to maintain full control over the corporations while the corporations were given an area of limited autonomy within which they could operate. This period is seen as a period where capital is fully organized within state strictures. The last phase, which the authors feel is contemporary, occurs as corporations become multinational. States are no longer able to fully control the activities of corporations because the corporations are able to shift their organizational, financial and productive activities back and forth between various states as laws governing their activities are found to be counterproductive or unprofitable to the corporation.

This is the "end of organized capital" as capital manages to escape the state's organization, although it maintains full control of itself and articulates a group of individuals responding to its own set of confines and strictures, the corporate service class (Lash and Urry, 1-17, see also chs. 2 and 7).

The most important aspect of Lash's and Urry's thesis is its recognition of the play of quasi-nomadic groups within the formal strictures of the state. Deleuze and Guattari theorize that although the state is able to lay down social and spatial bounds within and through which people under state control live and function, it also "captures" within its organization groups which enunciate themselves in a nomadic fashion, i.e., which are able to avoid, circumvent or escape state strictures and bounds.

> The outside appears simultaneously in two directions: huge worldwide machines branched out over the entire *ecumenon* at a given moment, which enjoy a large measure of autonomy in relation to the States for example, commercial organization of the 'multinational' type, or industrial complexes, or even religious formations . . . but also local mechanisms of bands, margins, minorities, which continue to affirm the rights of segmentary societies in opposition to the organs of State power. The modern world can provide us today with particularly well developed images of these two directions: worldwide ecumenical machines, but also a neoprimitivism, a new tribal society as described by Marshall McLuhan. (Deleuze and Guattari 1987: 360)

The advent of a corporate service class as a function of the disorganization of capital is in fact the articulation of a nomadic structure ("huge worldwide machines branched out over the entire *ecumenon* at a given moment") that is able to circumvent the politico-legal strictures of the state. Lash and Urry (1987: 161-162) argue that the corporate service class exists outside of state bounds insofar as its work space, its referent point, is the multinational or global corporation. As such the corporate service class consists of individuals who articulate themselves within a structure that is able to shift across state boundaries, through different social structures, indeed across geographical impediments, *at will* (Lash and Urry, ch. 7), and which sees the state as a structural impediment to its movement.[12] Lash and Urry conclude,

The state is subject to 'overloading' by the demands that are made of it by the very many interest groups which are often made up of, or led by, the service class; and at the same time the state is experienced as something to be struggled against since it is 'over-strong', unrepresentative, or overly bureaucratic. (Lash and Urry, 195)

The corporate service class, because of its location within an organization that spatially and socially supersedes the boundaries of the modern state, acts as a deterritorializing force within the state's organization. Through its articulation as a group which sits *partially* outside state control —given that its members are still citizens of one state or another, and that members of this class still encounter the exigency of movement and organization across state boundaries and around state strictures—the corporate service class is located in a tension within and against the social and spatial confines of the modern state. This tension calls into question the social, spatial and ontological siting of individuals within the modern state.

Thus the state must now cope to reintegrate elements of this nomadic force—the corporate service class, and its organizing forces, the multinational and global corporations—within a new series of social and spatial maps. Consequently the modern state must introduce synchronic change into its structures and strictures; that is to say, the state must introduce forms of mobility and rearticulation into its social fabric at the moment of its existence, rather than historically or *between* two moments of its development. The state has always been able to account for diachronic change, which it can relegate to a legitimating sphere in its history. But given that this struggle to reincorporate nomadic forms occurs after the state has already incorporated movement and change within its social and spatial fabric, the state is left with no other alternative but to introduce a reterritorialization—a redrawing of its social and spatial maps— enunciating a teleology, without appealing to the ameliorative function of history.

4. Emilio Ambasz: the Desituation of Subject and Place

With Emilio Ambasz one enters into a dialogue that does not problematize the siting of the individual subject. Ambasz's innovation is to nullify the question of space/subjectivity, indeed to create an architecture whose main function is to reconceive tectonic space so that the ontological priority of place in the spatial siting of subjectivity declines. This can be seen diachronically through the corpus of Ambasz's work in the continually intensifying fragmentation of the architectural object. It can also be seen within individual projects, as Ambasz seeks to develop the notion of an unstriated space where subjectivity is increasingly written with fewer and fewer narrative poles as spaces of orientation and segregation, within the work. This is a result of the conclusion present within each of Ambasz's works that the inherent contradiction within the formula space=place/movement is still present within the solution space=movement. For Ambasz, the solution is the negation of the concept of space itself and with it, the problem of the relation of the subject to a sited central subjectivity. This is resolved by rewriting Le Corbusier's final formula, space=movement, into the facticity of movement, thus formally negating the concept of space as a situational entity or environment.

The project for a *Casa de Retiro Espiritual* splinters the concept of structure—space—as a response to Le Corbusier's problematic surrounding structure and free movement. Here one is left with a fragment; two seemingly unsupported walls of a large room joined to establish the idea of a built place, but left open on two sides and standing free. The actual house (*Casa*) is underground, where two walls extend themselves vertically through ground level to create the fragment and with it a free plan much more unsettling than Le Corbusier's; the freeness of pure space, outside of territory. This is the ultimate free plan; both subjectivity and techtonic construct are sited within an almost unlimited (thus almost smooth) space. Here the ontological ground, the house, submerges beneath a perfectly smooth veldt which is completely free of striations that mark not only the state's construction, but also the limits within which formal subjectivity operates.

Ambasz establishes this first break with the modern discourse having critiqued space through the tactic of fragmentation. But the space of this critique is also the space of memory because one can still ponder the isolated remains of past discursive categories. The fragment, occupying a space of *freed* subjectivity and *diegetically dissolving* socius acts as an historical agent, and because of this, the *Casa* maintains an ambiguous

Fragment as narrative pole: *Casa de Retiro Espiritual*
(photo courtesy of the author)

character. On the one hand, it remains as an isolated pole within an undifferentiated narrative, which leaves open the possibility of the creation of a differentiated space within an unstructured plane. Ambasz does not capitalize on this possibility. On the other hand, the solitary fragment found at the *Casa* can also serve to reinflate narratives and their attendant constructions of spatial and social order. After all, the single piece coincides too neatly with the underground structure, thus enabling it to represent not only fragmentation but also its exact reverse, the imminent establishment of order; one could complete the open sides above ground following the strictures enunciated by the house below the ground.[14]

The *Schlumberger Research Laboratories* project continues the *Casa's* theme of fragmentation but also introduces the free play of multiplicities within an environment of flux. Like the *Casa*, there is both an underground structure and surface fragments. Unlike the *Casa*, the multiplicity of both the fragments (their shapes and materiality) and the various functions of the spaces below ground do not allow for singular readings. While the *Casa* can allow for a singular subject position (i.e. outside of the fragment, viewing the fragment), the lab complex creates a site of dispersion. Here the structure below, the labs, does not create a ground for the fragments which allows for the assignation of signification upon the piece. Rather, the heterogeneity within the lab complex sets up a field of potential as opposed to the binary logic of ground/not ground that the *Casa* rests upon.

The lab project, then, sits in a field without memory; it does not reflect on the shattering of what was once a statistical whole, as did the *Casa*, but instead already takes as its point of departure an undifferentiated social field. Fragmentation is not a tactic, but an ontological force or condition. The fragments above ground act as a series of randomly placed magnetic poles which do nothing to site the subject. Rather they place one within a shifting field of potentials where the subject moves towards the nomadic end of its continuum,[15] moving from pole to pole, always repelled at the moment of arrival. Perception within this field is not diegetic but schizophrenic. "What the schizophrenic experiences, both as an individual and as a member of the human species, is not at all any one specific aspect of nature, but nature as the process of production" (Deleuze and Guattari 1983: 3). What one experiences as a nomad within a field of potentialities is the endless production of these possibilities as one

Space contra memory: *Schlumberger Research Labs* as a field of polarities
(photo courtesy of the author)

moves from pole to pole. This production, insofar as it may be seen serially through one's movement around the fragments, is neither ordered nor predetermined. Rather it follows rules of chance and ad hoc observation and as such, "overtakes all idealistic categories and constitutes a cycle whose relationship to desire is that of an immanent principle" (Deleuze and Guattari 1983: 5).

5. Politics in a Desituated Space

If one takes Ambasz's projects to be a serious commentary on the state of the socius in contemporary life then several conclusions of political importance to a left—or progressive—political agenda must be made: first, no such agenda will have any effect as long as it attempts to operate through[16] some form of static political site. Here, then, Laclau's and Mouffe's privileging of hegemony as a political tactic runs to despair. Hegemony, according to Laclau and Mouffe, occupies a theoretical void in alternative politics. That void was once filled by the romantic notions of spontaneity and revolution that went with what Laclau and Mouffe (1985: chs 1, 2 and 4) would call Marxism's monistic privileging of production and of the proletariat as the proper environment and subject of history. Tactically, hegemony replaces the privileged space of the proletariat with a knitting together of an oppositional fabric comprised of various alternative groups and their political agendas (Mouffe 1988: 89-91)—among them the ecological movements, feminism, movements for racial equality, guest workers' movements in Europe, etc.

Hegemony takes on the spatial characteristic of a constructed space in which various political discourses come to articulate themselves within one general agenda—democracy—based on a principle of "radical" equality, and through the articulation of a single political site based upon reciprocity. Indeed, Mouffe has described the hegemonic relation as

an ensemble of relatively *stable* social forms, the *materialization* of a social articulation in which different social relations *react reciprocally either to provide each other with mutual conditions of existence*, or at least to neutralize the potentially destructive effects of certain social relations on the reproduction of other such relations. (Mouffe 1988: 90, emphasis added)

A successful hegemonic operation articulates a new social space, which would, then, unfold over the socius and rearticulate a sociospatial fabric in which various political struggles have become addressed and have made their weight felt upon the social structures of the state. However, this duplicates the spatial problems seen in the earlier discussion of Beaux Arts space and Lyotard's reciprocating/centered subject: Laclau and Mouffe reconceive a stable political space where the hegemonic operation tends towards stability and reciprocity, but they fail to take into account the fact that reciprocity is inherently inimical to stability. In combination the two concepts tend towards dissociation. Laclau and Mouffe return to a liberalism which is part and parcel with Beaux Arts space and a narrative mechanics relying on the unmediated subject for their progression. But these are inherently unsuited for a socius within which dissociation is an ontological ground. The chain of correspondences that Laclau and Mouffe see as a necessary series of linkages amongst and between groups struggling to articulate a political project or agenda creates a linearity around the enunciation of a specific and limited avenue of political dialogue and intervention which mirrors Le Corbusier's transit networks and subjects itself to Harvey's critique of the linear infrastructures and the exigencies of capital/industrial production. According to Harvey (1985: 150), linear avenues of discourse and movement serve to reproduce the "chronic instability of regional and spatial configurations, a tension within the geography of accumulation and between fixity and motion, between the rising power to overcome space and the immobile spatial structures required for such a purpose." How, then, can one conceive of stability as a progressive, or leftist, political tactic when (a) the polity will not sit still long enough for the stability to ground itself; and (b) the enunciated stability is nothing more than the tired rehashing of the claims of the existing structure of the present political discourse?

The second consequence to be drawn from Ambasz's sociocritique is that the political right understands dissociation all too well, and operates one step ahead of both the theoretical and the political left. Grossberg has argued that the right employs a political tactic similar to hegemony which he chooses to call "disciplined mobilizations." As with hegemonic operations, disciplined mobilizations create social spaces for interaction. Unlike hegemonic space, however, disciplined mobilizations do not articulate a stable or linear political space; they are without stable spatial enunciation and social structuration.[17] Instead, disciplined mobilizations operate by patching together socially disarticulated fragments around the emotional magnetization of specific symbols and social practices (Grossberg 1988: 35-40). They operate through the articulation of social economies of emotion, desire and nostalgia. Here emotionally charged symbols are suffused with political content within "cultural" spaces and places that would not normally seem to be open to overt political coding: Thus a rock concert reaffirms the nostalgic glory of the american way of life; advertising links the flag to the desire to consume; economic crises are used to rearticulate nostalgic notions of nation and social hierarchy.[18] And all of these are then linked to various conservative agendas and political programs.

Characteristically a disciplined mobilization occurs through *the event*: a rock concert, an advertisement, a film, and, on a scale of longer duration, a "generally perceived" crisis such as the economic problems besieging the United Kingdom. The underlying character of the event is temporality and instability. Emotional suffusion is not an easily sustainable tactic; thus the right assumes a politics akin to Ambasz's nomadic fields through the perpetual creation of temporally bounded scenes of emotion and politics—sites that perpetuate movement—that do not allow for either rest or sustained dialogue. Even general social crises are temporally bounded by the solution offered through the mobilization.

A third consequence is that the left must adopt this tactic and begin to counterpose its own symbols across and through those of the right—in a form of field reversal—at all opportunities. Witness a recent series of advertisements in the *New York Times*: adopting some of the right's favorite symbols—the home, the family, order under the law—and its favorite nemesis—"drug gangs"—a gun control lobby argued that the immediate control of automatic weapons would severely limit the operational efficacy of these drug gangs since the guns come from the United States. Gun control would thus directly protect the security of the home and the safety of children in the streets. Here the emotion of security and the nostalgia for the stable nuclear family are affectively reversed against the right agenda and played across the momentary crises of drug shootings and violence in order to further a progressive political agenda *viz.* gun control.

Progressive political agendas will not be *effectively* articulated until they are *affectively* articulated. It has been the particular genius of the right to marry up the affectivity of emotion with the effectivity of a conservative political agenda. It now stands to the left to reverse this trend by reversing the symbolic fields in which the right operates by investing political symbols and cultural practices now commonly appropriated by the right with a progressive and alternative mobilizing affect to the fields presently at play.

In a recent news feature[19] discussing the rise of "dirty" political campaigning and the media tactics available to politicians one, media consultant noted that, presently, safe media campaigns meant "attack, attack without delay, attack in kind, do not appear to be uneager, or unwilling to attack." These are precisely the right's tactics *viz.* disciplined mobilizations and the politics of affect within the context of a shifted subjectivity. Merely substitute "code" for "attack" and one has the proper formula: code, code without delay, code in kind, do not appear to be uneager or unwilling to code. I want to argue that the political left must adopt this strategy through the following tactics: first, reinflate what have been traditional symbols of the american left with a significant level of affectivity. Second, suffuse popular events and cultural practices with these symbols; this must be done at all opportunities. The genius of the right is that it does not let up. Third, adopt the tactic of field reversals. Symbols used by the right can be subverted through their emotive use in left or progressively-oriented arguments. This last tactic has two beneficial effects; it not only subverts what has hitherto been a specific instance of conservative semiotics, it may also rearticulate a particular conservative agenda into a progressive one as the field reversal operates as a form of immanent critique.

I would like to thank Prof. Lawrence Grossberg for his timely advice and aid in the completion of this essay. His help enabled me to convert a series of disjointed conclusions and analyses into a coherent statement.

Notes

1. Having just said this, I will note that Paxton's Crystal Palace (London, 1850) is generally considered to be the first work of modern architecture, both structurally (steel with glass overlay) and in its enunciation of a free spatial plan.

2. Which manages to encode its principles in the founding declaration of the Congrès Internationaux d'Architecture Moderne (CIAM). See CIAM, 1928: 109-114 and 1933: 137-145.

3. As in Mies' German Pavilion at the Barcelona World Exhibition, 1929.

4. See, for instance, Le Corbusier's *Plan Obus*, 1930, for Algiers as a traffic hub for Africa and his plans for *La Ville Radieuse*, 1931, as a city designed under the principles of spatial segregation of function and high speed traffic links between spaces/functions. Both plans executed with Pierre Jeanneret.

5. See, for instance, Marx in the now famous passage from the *Communist Manifesto*:

> The bourgeoise cannot exist without constantly revolutionizing the instruments of production, and thereby the relations of production, and with them the whole relations of society. . . .
>
> The bourgeoise has subjected the country to the rule of the towns. It has created enormous cities, has greatly increased the urban population as compared with the rural, and has thus rescued a considerable part of the population from the idiocy of rural life. . . . It has agglomerated population, centralized means of production, and has concentrated property in a few hands. (Marx and Engels, 19-20)

Marshall Berman is in apparent agreement with this thesis when he argues that in fact what is essential to Marx as a modern writer is the fact that Marx theorizes through an epistemological framework of change as the underlying character of his thought, which Berman would perhaps characterize as *development* (1988: ch. 2).

Max Weber writes that

> What can be stated is the following: The urban local market with its exchange between agricultural and non-agricultural producers and local traders, its personal customer relationships, and its low-capital small shops, represents a kind of 'exchange-economy' counterpart to the 'exchangeless' internal economy of the *oikos*, which draws on systematically allocated service prestations and commodity deliveries of dependent specialized production units and integrates these activities from the manor. The *regulation* of the exchange and production conditions in the city represents the counterpart to the *coordination* of activities of the units combined on the economy of the *oikos*. . . . (*Economy and Society*, 1220-1221, all emphases in original)

Bataille, who, as Hollier (1988: viii) has noted, has all but disappeared from the sociological horizon, also observed this tension, but rather than marginalize, or radicalize its implications, as did Marx and Weber, he chose to use this as his theoretical starting point, thus enunciating a socius, that is always already in tension between individual and collectivity. From here the step to Deleuze and the turn to coding/recoding is easily seen. See Bataille (1988: 81), where he says,

As human beings we are not solely 'linked linear organisms': by and large we use part of our forces to break, partially or totally, the bonds that unite us with society, with the hope becoming free individuals. I propose to reserve the name 'person' for the compound being that results from this secondary action.

6. This then is the enunciation of the French (radical freedom) and German (radical unification) narrative strings of modernity as developed by Lyotard (ch. 9).

7. See, for instance, Le Corbusier's *Plan Voisin*, Paris, 1925, executed with Pierre Jeanneret.

8. Beaux Arts aesthetics situated space within the strictures of symmetric axes and as such brought a classical aesthetic order—with its inherent assumptions of social order, personal position, subjectivity, etc.—to what is commonly called early modern or Neo-Classical architecture. We see this, in fact, as late as the Rockefeller Center (Reinhard & Hofmeister, et al., New York, chiefly 1932-1939) and the Chrysler Building (Van Alen, New York, 1928-1930) to name just two buildings which spatially duplicate Beaux Arts space, but which, because of the form of their ornamentation, their size and rectilinear form, are given a place within the discourse of modern architecture with the trumped-up term, Art Deco.

9. It is worthy to note that towards the end of his career Le Corbusier seems to have rethought the problematic concerning space, embarking on what seems to be a panic project to rearticulate both space and subjectivity based upon the formula *space=nostalgia*, which, as Ross (1988: 120) has noted of the Frankfurt School, situated Le Corbusier within an "economy of value, wherein value is produced through the vehicle of nostalgia and where value is measured solely by the relative coherence of erosion of folk experience." His Cathedral at Ronchamp, the Indian capitol at Chandigarh and the Maisons Jaoul all reinject the narrative pole of subjectivity through two tactics: first, Le Corbusier attempts to revive place through a reassertion of tectonic form related to the place of the construction. Second, the attempts to reinscribe a narrative over the place through the tactile variation of the concrete pours within each site; some are rough, some smooth, some slatted, etc. In this way, points within the site are to be seen as differentiated, with subject theoretically gaining a sense of difference between, thus narrative across, different locations in the structure, This latter tactic, the variation of material and form within the piece in order to gain a sense of the narrative that the particular place may impart upon the user coincides with Frampton's reading of Aalto's Säynatsalo Town Hall (1983: 28-30).

10. In a manifesto entitled "Working Theses" (1923: 74) which appeared in a constructivist journal entitled *G*, Mies wrote,

> Not yesterday, not tomorrow, only today can be given form.
> Only this architecture creates.
> Create form out of the nature of the task with the means of our time. This is our work.

O F F I C E   B U I L D I N G

11. Indeed, it may be said that capital is in need of a constantly shifting social body in order to reabsorb its surplus in a series of changing projects and products that meet the needs of this changing social body.

12. Lash's and Urry's analysis, insofar as it enumerates a specific social/structural phenomenon within the development of the modern state is quite correct. Where they fault, however, is in the final chapter of their book, Chapter 9, "Postmodern Culture and Disorganized Capitalism: Some Conclusions." Here Lash and Urry attempt to understand the problem of postmodern aesthetics as an instance of legitimation of the corporate service class. Two things need to be said of this: first, it is problematic to introduce the concept of legitimation, a concept properly relegated to earlier social formations, to a genuine mutation within a state structure which *itself no longer employs legitimation as a means of self-articulation.* In this respect, the authors are anachronistic. Second, the authors discuss postmodern culture as if it were simply the reflection of underlying social formations which are autonomous from the cultural sphere and in fact with are reflected by the cultural sphere. Needless to say, this type of reflection theory is highly problematic, and, given the current debate over the force and formation of the cultural sphere of social life, cannot be taken seriously.

13. The concentration of this analysis upon the corporate service class should not cause it to be seen as the only nomadic group within contemporary state bounds. Indeed, the shifts in a state's map which allow for—and in fact are in part caused by the growth of—any single nomadic formation, *qua* their nature as shifts, will allow for the growth of other nomadic structures as the redrawing of the state's margins and the shifts in its boundaries create gasp and openings which are not immediately filled, thus allowing for nomadic growth.

14. Thus Ambasz tracks himself along Lacan's words "That no signification can be sustained other than by reference to another signification" (1977: 150). The signification of the fragment is void except with reference to the house below, which thus serves, although unwittingly, as a significatory (thus ontological) ground to the fragment above it.

15. I am grateful to Larry Grossberg for pointing out the concept of nomadic subjectivity within the *Schlumberger Research Laboratories* project.

16. Political agendas, as with all other ideal phenomena, do not articulate themselves across a single space or time. Rather they chart trajectories across social formations and the spaces that these formations occupy in time.

17. Although it argues an ontological positions quite similar to that of Laclau and Mouffe.

18. This last moment, of course, is the Thatcherist agenda as described by Stuart Hall.

19. CBS Evening News, 5 November 1989.

References

Ambasz, Emilio. (1988). *The Poetics of the Pragmatic* New York: Rizzoli.

Bataille, Georges and Roger Callois. (1988). "Sacred Sociology and the Relationship between 'Society,' 'Organism,' and 'Being.'" *The College of Sociology* (1937-39). Ed. Denis Hollier. Trans. Betsy Wing. Minneapolis: University of Minnesota Press.

Berman, Marshall. (1988). *All That is Solid Melts into Air: The Experience of Modernity.* New York: Penguin Books.

Congrès Internationaux d'Architecture Moderne (CIAM). (1928). "La Sarraz déclaration." *Programs and Manifestos on Twentieth Century Architecture.* Ed. Ulrich Conrads. Trans. Michael Bullock. 1987: Cambridge, MA: MIT Press.

———. (1933). "Charter of Athens: Tenets." *Programs and Manifestos on Twentieth Century Architecture.* Ed. Ulrich Conrads. Trans. Michael Bullock. 1987: Cambridge, MA: MIT Press.

Conrads, Ulrich, ed. (1987). *Programs and Manifestoes on Twentieth Century Architecture.* Trans. Michael Bullock. Cambridge, MA: MIT Press.

Deleuze, Gilles, and Felix Guattari. (1983). *Anti-Oedipus: Capitalism and Schizophrenia.* Trans. Robert Hurley, Mark Seem and Helen Lane. Minneapolis: University of Minnesota Press.

———. (1987). *A Thousand Plateaus: Capitalism and Schizophrenia.* Trans. Brian Massumi. Minneapolis: University of Minnesota Press.

Frampton, Kenneth. (1983). "Towards a Critical Regionalism: Six Points for an Architecture of Resistance." *The Anti-Aesthetic: Essays on Postmodern Culture.* Ed. Hal Foster. Port Townsend, WA: The Bay Press.

Giedion, Siegfried. (1975). *Mechanization Takes Command: A Contribution to Anonymous History.* New York: W. W. Norton.

Grossberg, Lawrence, et. al. (1988). *It's a Sin: Essays on Postmodernism Politics and Culture.* Sydney: Power Publications.

Harvey, David. (1985). "The Geopolitics of Capitalism." *Social Relations and Spatial Structures.* Eds. Derek Gregory and John Urry. New York: St Martin's Press.

Hollier, Denis. (1988). "Foreword: Collage." *The College of Sociolog (1937-39).* Trans. Betsy Wing. Minneapolis: University of Minnesota Press.

Lacan, Jacques. (1977). "The Agency of the Letter in the Unconscious or Reason Since Freud." *Ecrits: A Selection.* Trans. A. M. Sheridan. New York: W. W. Norton.

Laclau, Ernesto, and Chantal Mouffe. (1985). *Hegemony and Socialist Strategy: Towards a Radical Democratic Politics.* London: Verso Books.

Lash, Scott and John Urry. (1987). *The End of Organized Capitalism.* Madison, WI: The University of Wisconsin Press.

Lyotard, Jean-François. (1984). *The Postmodern Condition: A Report on Knowledge.* Trans. Geoff Bennington and Brian Massumi. Minneapolis: University of Minnesota Press.

Marx, Karl and Frederick Engels. (1954). *The Communist Manifesto.* Chicago: Henry Regnery Company.

Mouffe, Chantal. (1988). "Hegemony and New Political Subjects: Toward a New Concept of Democracy." Trans. Stanley Gray. *Marxism and the Interpretation of Culture*. Eds. Lawrence Grossberg and Cary Nelson. Urbana, IL: University of Illinois Press.

Ross, Andrew. (1988). "The Work of Nature in the Age of Electronic Emission." *Social Text*, 18: 116-128.

Rowe, Colin. (1976). "The Mathematics of the Ideal Villa." *The Mathematics of the Ideal Villa and Other Essays*. Cambridge, MA: MIT Press.

Sant'Elia, Antonio and Filippo Tommaso Marinetti. (1914). "Futurist Architecture." *Programs and Manifestos on Twentieth Century Architecture*. Ed. Ulrich Conrads. Trans. Michael Bullock. 1987: Cambridge, MA: MIT Press.

Van der Rohe, Mies. (1923). "Working Theses." *Programs and Manifestos on Twentieth Century Architecture*. Ed. Ulrich Conrads. Trans. Michael Bullock. 1987: Cambridge, MA: MIT Press.

Weber, Max. (1978). *Economy and Society*, vol. 2. Eds. Guenther Roth and Claus Wittich. Trans. Ephraim Fischoff, et al. Los Angeles: University of California Press.

(photo by Robert Merrill and Maria Hall)
Federal Trade Commission Building, Pennsylvania and Constitution Avenues

This building faces the Canadian Embassy and exhibits the solidity and centeredness that are absent in the Embassy's design (*see* p. viii above). The interplay between a sign which purports to contain and enclose its own meaning and one which obviously de-centers that whole concept raises the question of architecture as cultural vandalism. In its location among the great monuments to American ideology, the Canadian Embassy is built graffiti, a monument to emptiness (*see* p. 167 below).

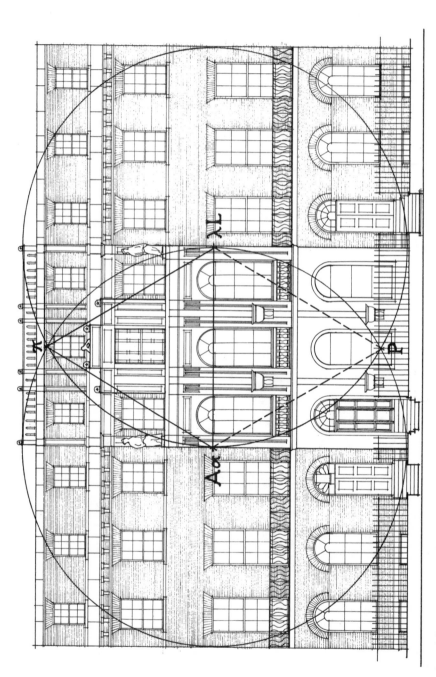

Vesica picis, an apparatus for generating equilateral triangles, superimposed on the façades of Nos. 12-13-14 Lincoln's Inn Fields. This construction suggests the rational man, but within the central No. 13 is the feminine triangle, *alpha-lambda-pi* or Anna Livia Plurabelle, the *anima* in Joyce's *Finnegan's Wake.* (*drawing courtesy of the author*)

In

The

Museyroom

Jennifer Bloomer

**Architecture
University of Florida**

"THIS IS THE HOUSE and museum of SIR JOHN SOANE, R. A., architect. Soane was born in 1753, the son of a small country builder, and died, after a long and distinguished career, in 1837. He lived here for the last twenty-four years of his life (1813-37). Previously, he had lived next door in No. 12, which he had designed for himself in 1792. This and the corresponding house on the east (No. 14) are both Soane's work, and the three houses together make a balanced composition towards the fields."[1]

"THIS IS the way to the museyroom. Mind your hats goan in!"(*FW*, 8.10)[2] Through the looking glass: emerge from the dark concavity out onto the convex surface. Where you are is where you are going. Bull's-eye! "Now yiz are in the Willingdone Museyroom"(*FW*, 8.10).

At five o'clock in the morning on 18 March 1788, the twenty-four-year-old student John Soane set out from London to Italy. Some months later, braving his poor Italian, he presented himself at the studio of Giovanbattista Piranesi in Rome. Piranesi, eaten up with an unspeakable disease and weeks away from the end of four decades of frenzied line drawing, was apparently impressed. Soane carried away with him four large engravings from the *Views of Rome*.

"THIS IS the Hausman all paven and stoned, that cribbed the Cabin that never was owned that cocked his leg and hennad his Egg" (*FW*, 205.34-35).

THIS IS the Picture Room. This is a hidden compartment. This wall swings out. Behind this wall is another that swings out. On the other side of this swinging wall you can see the etchings of Piranesi, "one of the two greatest architectural draughtsmen of the eighteenth century" (*Lincoln's Inn Guidebook*).

John Soane kept Piranesi in the closet. If we slice through Nos. 12 and 13 *Lincoln's Inn Fields* (a Liffey kind of place), we can see a resemblance to "32 West 11th streak" that goes far beyond the numerical identity of address (which, in addition to the acronymic point of resemblance, the architect of the latter would have found highly significant).[3] When an architect makes a drawing to represent what would lie before the eye were the object sliced and a piece removed, s/he depicts the "cut" surfaces of material by scratching lines or marking spots, working these surfaces until they appear as dark figures upon a light ground. We call the technique *pocher*, the etymology of which suggests black spots before the eye. We have also come to call the form represented *poché*, particularly when it is complex or when it contains vesicles or crypts. The Piranesi scratchings are contained within the *poché* of the house that Soane built.

We call the drawing itself a section. A section is not a mirroring construction, but a kind of text that has been lifted out (dissected), a text that can then be read, that is, misread or rewritten. The information provided by the section is always incomplete. "And look at this prepronominal *funferal*, engraved and retouched and edgewiped and puddenpadded, very like a whale's egg farced with pemmican, as were it sentenced to be nuzzled over a full trillion times for ever and a night till his noddle sink or swim by that ideal reader suffering from an ideal insomnia: all those red raddled obeli cayennepeppercast over the text, calling unnecessary attention to errors, omissions, repetitions, and misalignments . . ." (*FW*, 120.09-16).

If we dissect out the pattern of letter T's from *Finnegans Wake*, we have one of the important generative sections of the work. Triple tapped *poché*. T. T. T. Beams on posts. Trabeation. Patterns of black marks in front of the eye. Apparatus. "One cannot help noticing that rather more than half of the lines run north-south in the Nemzes and Bukarahast directions while the others go west-east in search from Maliziies with Bulgarad for, tiny tot though it looks when schtschupnistling alongside other incunabula, it has its cardinal points for all that" (*FW*, 114.02-07).

The *poché* at No. 13 is not uniform on the vertical. There are strange disjunctions, holes in this architecture: slivers of space, shafts of light. There is here an intangible but sensible construction that exists within the material construction. "Soane designed this house to live in, but also as a setting for his antiquities and works of art" (Lincoln's Inn *Guidebook*). Walter Benjamin in his *The Origin of German Tragic Drama* cites Johann Ritter on language:

> IN reality the whole of creation is language, and so is literally created by the word, the created and creating word itself. . . . But the letter is inextricably bound up with this word both in general and in particular. . . . All the plastic arts, architecture, sculpture, painting, etc., belong pre-eminently among such script, and developments and derivations of it.[4]

ALLEGORY: texts read through other texts; fragmentary, partial, hieroglyphic, ambiguous; paradigm of palimpsest; critical in the involvement of a misreading; disregard for aesthetic boundaries, especially that between the visual and verbal; "piling up of fragments ceaselessly"; emerging from "an appreciation of the transience of things, and the concern to rescue them for eternity."[5]

Fredric Jameson distinguishes Walter Benjamin's concept of allegory from the traditional one:

> The allegorical spirit is profoundly discontinuous, a matter of breaks and heterogeneities, of the multiple polysemia of the dream rather than the homogeneous representation of the symbol. Our traditional concept of allegory . . . [is] a one-dimensional view of this signifying process, which might only be set in motion and complexified were we willing to entertain the more alarming notion that such equivalences are themselves in constant change and transformation at each perpetual present of the text.[6]

THIS IS the Dressing Room, a small room that connects the Study to the Corridor. Surmounting the dispersion of antique marbles, Renaissance bronzes, and small pictures, above either of the two facing doorways, are busts of Andrea Palladio and Inigo Jones. Soane's formidable fathers, looking down upon him, far below and naked. The anxiety of influence concretized and embedded in the construction. "Allegorical personification has always concealed the fact that its function is not the personification of things, but rather to give the concrete a more imposing form by getting it up as a person" (Benjamin 1977: 187).

THIS IS the Monument Yard, a tiny court at the heart of the Museum.

"Mememormee!" (*FW*, 628.14).

IN its fully developed, baroque form allegory brings with it its own court; the profusion of emblems is grouped around the figural center, which is never absent from genuine allegories, as opposed to periphrases of concepts. They seem to be arranged in an arbitrary way: *The confused 'court'*—the title of a Spanish *Trauerspiel*—could be adopted as the model of allegory. This court is subject to the law of 'dispersal' and 'collectedness.' (Benjamin 1977: 188)

THIS IS the Breakfast Room. John Soane wrote, "The views from this room into the Monument Court and into the Museum, the mirrors in the ceiling, and the looking-glasses, combined with the variety of outline and general arrangement and the design and decoration of this limited space, present a succession of those fanciful effects which constitute the poetry of architecture."[7] In this house, Soane anticipates Roman Jakobson: the poetic as the projection of the metaphoric axis onto the metonymic, the intersection of synchrony and diachrony. It is the superimposition of a dissemination and an emplotment. "The letter! The litter!" (*FW*, 93.24). "Problem ye ferst, construct ann aquilittoral dryankle Probe loom! With his primal handstoe in his sole salivarium. Concoct an equoangular trilitter. [As Rhombulus and Rhebus went building rhomes one day]" (*FW*, 286.19-22 and n. 1).

THIS IS the Dome, the central area of the Museum. "This, already completed while Soane was living at No. 12 and therefore the oldest part of the present Museum, is a kind of Grotto of Antiquities, perhaps inspired by the romantic engravings of G.B. Piranesi" (Lincoln's Inn *Guidebook*). "From this brilliantly lit room, Light filters down to the ground floor, and, on the north, still further down to the otherwise completely obscure Crypt. . . ."[8]

THIS IS the Crypt. It is a dark place, the underground chamber, the vesicle, the secret place, the place of secretions. "All he could see was a labyrinth of lines crossing and recrossing each other, which covered the paper so thickly that it was difficult to discern the blank spaces between them. 'Read it,' said the officer. 'I can't,' said the explorer. 'Yet it's clear enough,' said the officer."[9]

In the year in which Soane began work on No. 13, Johann Wilhelm Ritter wrote,

> IN THE context of allegory the image is only a signature, only the monogram of essence, not the essence itself in a mask. But there is nothing subordinate about written script; it is not cast away in reading, like dross. It is absorbed along with what is read, as its 'pattern.' (cited in Benjamin 1977: 214-215)

THIS IS the priest all shaven and shorn, that roundheaded Neapolitan with the circular signature: Jack Vico, who could no more reconcile his circle with the square of Descartes than could his devotee, Jack Piranesi, two decades later, or the academicians two centuries later. The problem of squaring the circle would be left to Jack Joyce. In the house that Jack built, the squares are not squares and the circles are not circles. "For I've flicked up all the crambs as they crumbed from your table um, singing glory allaloserem, cog it out, here goes a sum. So read we in must book. It tells. He prophets most who bilks the best" (FW, 304.35-305.02)[10]

"IN order for a part of the past to be touched by the present, there must be no continuity between them."[11]

"Is the strays world moving mound or what static babel is this, tell us?" (FW, 499.33-34).

> IN THE wide space of architecture, that which is not the building is of no consequence. Ideas, descriptions, critiques, theories, even ideology—all abstractions—are, in the end, passive and inert, the ether of the architectural space. The object—separate and privileged—is the sole subject of an enclosed and centripetal order. Architecture is a collection of ruins that closes at six o'clock.[12]

The museum is the place of preservation of the dead, the authoritative, the valued. It is the place of the power of the Father. (John Soane, the Master Builder, bitterly disappointed with the way his two sons conducted their lives, de-soaned them by leaving his house as a museum of architecture.) The muses are invisible, hiding away in the poché. The museum is quiet, static, clean.

But *this* museum is full of junk, full of debris, fragmented and untidy, "like a children's nursery" (Benjamin 1977: 188). The House O'Shea or O'Shame:

> The warped flooring of the lair and soundconducting walls thereof, to say nothing of the uprights and imposts, were persianly literatured with burst loveletters, telltale stories, stickyback snaps, doubtful eggshells, bouchers, flints, borers, puffers, amygdaloid almonds, rindless raisins, alphybettyformed verbage, vivlical viasses, ompiter dictas, visus umbique, ahems and ahahs, imeffible tries at speech unasyllabled, you owe mes, eyoldhums, fluefoul smut, fallen lucifers, vestas which had served, showered ornaments, borrowed brogues, reversibles jackets, blackeye lenses, family jars, falsehair shirts, Godforsaken scapulars, neverworn breeches, cutthroat ties, counterfeit franks, best intentions, curried notes, upset latten tintacks, unused mill and stumpling stones, twisted quills, painful digests, magnifying wineglasses, solid objects cast at goblins, once current puns, quashed quotatoes, messes of mottage, unquestionable issue papers, seedy ejaculations. . . ."
> (*FW*, 193.08-23)

"IN THE ruin history has physically merged into the setting. And in this guise history does not assume the form of the process of an eternal life so much as that of irresistible decay" (Benjamin 1977: 177).

IN THE Picture Room, high up, you will note a painting by Sir Francis Bourgeois, entitled *A Hen Defending Her Chickens*.

"THIS IS the jinnies with their legahorns feinting to read in their handmade's book of stralegy while making their war undisides the Willingdone" (*FW*, 8.31-33).

THIS IS "the hen that crowed on the turrace of Babel" (*FW*, 199.30).

(After six o'clock) the chickens enter the House to eat the malt. They peck, they hatch, they cackle, they scratch, they mess things up. They produce objectionable odors.

THIS IS the Hatchery. It is a place of production, flow, desire, signifiers on the cheep. It is chaotic, dynamic, dirty. There is no author-ity. It is the place of hatching—hatching lines of *poché*—and the place of hatches —small doors opening into dark places. The gesture of hatching a drawing is also a kitchen gesture: the French verb *hacher* denotes both these things, as well as the act of hacking something to bits. The hatchery bears the trace of architectural terrorism, "as sure as herself pits hen to paper and there's scribings scrawled on eggs" (*FW*, 615.09-10). Here, in this smooth space, plots are hatched.

"Rockaby, babel, flatten a wall" (*FW*, 278.04).

"A feminist architecture is not architecture at all."[13]

THIS IS the House That Jill (*ou Gilles, peut-être?*) Built. ("Which title is the true-to-type motto-in-lieu for that Tick for Teac thatchment painted witt wheth one darkness . . ?") *FW*, 139.29-30).

"Tip. (Bullseye! Game!) How Copenhagen ended. This way the museyroom. Mind your boots goan out" (*FW*, 10.21-23).

Here, the house of Soane slides into identity with Joyce's Willingdone Museyroom, the museum which, again, is simultaneously the locus of preservation and exhibition of objects of historical value and a place of flow. In Joyce, the joint is the naming of the battle of Waterloo, where the museum of the "Lipoleum" and the "Willingdone" slips into the place of micturition and excrement (the hatchery). For the textual construction here, the joint between Joyce's museum and Soane's is the *vesica piscis*, or fish's bladder, with all puns intended.

Postscript

The drawing presented here as a frontispiece is a superimposition of the façade of Nos. 12-13-14 Lincoln's Inn Fields and a diagram that appears on page 293 of *Finnegans Wake*. The diagram is the *vesica piscis*, a Euclidean apparatus for the generation of an equilateral triangle. This apparatus is effected by means of the compasses, the instrument and invention of the architect and the instrument of authority. The diagram itself is emblematic of rational man; but inscribed within, and in the superimposition over and bounding the central No. 13, is the feminine triangle, designated *alpha-lambda-pi*, or ALP, the initials of Anna Livia Plurabelle, the feminine figure of the *Wake*.

The text constructed here sets up the duality of the museum (the place of the preservation of objects assigned value by an authority, and a hallowed architectural type) and the hatchery (a kind of construction, but not an architectural type, a concept that is figured by generative processes) and poses Soane's house (a collection of architectural debris) as the interface. The crypt is the critical joint. It belongs to the museum, but is a monad of the hatchery: a mined field, a holey space, vessel of the nomad. The inscriptions (the encrypted) of the hatchery undermine the foundations of the museum.

Another joint is the bull's eye. The museum is entered through the prominent and disorienting bull's-eye mirror on Soane's stair and exited (through Joyce's text) with the exclamation "Bullseye! Game!" that closes the "Museyroom" section of *Finnegans Wake*. The connections of the bull's eye, the mirror, the strange *poché* of Soane, and the literary (or litterary) *poché* of Joyce's letter constitute one of the structural systems of this text. We might call this a section—a concept that swerves from the Vitruvian concept of *scenographia* (which depends on an idea of the eye as instrument of the gaze, rather than as encrypted flow). This section can be approximated by two appropriations. One is from Jurij Lotman: "a construction of a pattern of intersections" (intersections here defined as ruptures in a system that mark its collision with another system). The other, intersecting neatly with the first, is from Marcel Duchamp: "*un Repos capable de pires excentricités*" (a rest capable of the worst eccentricities).

Other examples of such sections are the constellations "THIS IS" and "IN THE." "THIS IS" is a metonymical figure of "The House That Jack Built" (which connects Joyce and John Ruskin through the labyrinth of the nursery rhyme);[14] mirroring Joyce's "museyroom" section, it serves, at the same time, as a form of structural *poché* for the textual construction here. "IN THE" signifies enterability by the reader. It also refers to the grand allegorical construction of Walter Benjamin, the *Passagen Werk*. (The "IN" is also the "N" that provides the *poché* of Benjamin's construction, and some "IN" appropriations that appear here are lifted from the "N" of the *Passagen Werk*.)

It is architecture's resistance to narrativity that suggests the possibility of a relationship to allegory, which indicates both form and technique, which hovers between sign and symbol and between the embrace of history and its denial, a counternarrative (but not antinarrative) device. Because of its relationship to temporality, narrative itself is uniquely literary. Yet, as Paul Ricoeur points out, its trace remains in the concept of emplotment. The plot described by Ricoeur smacks of the architectonic. The plot of which he writes is architecture, though not building. Besides being architectonic constructions, plots, like architecture, are both singular and nonsingular, both submissive to paradigms and deviant from established models, both conform to tradition and rebel against paradigms from the tradition.[15] It is this concept of emplotment—with its relationship to structure—that will allow for a countering of simplistic (metaphorical) notions of narrative in architecture without disposing of the idea altogether.

In literary texts in which the chronological structure of narrative is faded or indistinct, the reader must construct the narrative by sifting through the debris of the text. In these works (good examples are Thomas Pynchon's *V* and Vladimir Nabokov's *Pale Fire*), meaning resides in relationships of parts and structures, or apparatus, of the text, rather than in explicit narrative content. At the point where meaning lies not in a one-to-one relationship between thing and concept, but in the constructive operation upon many possible relationships at many levels of scale (letter, word, sentence, paragraph, plot), the literary work not only begins to bear a resemblance to architecture (which is "illegible" in a similar way that such texts are "illegible"), but also becomes a model of what architecture might be.[16]

In *Finnegans Wake* the operations that necessarily bound a text—writing and reading—constitute the substance of the text to such a degree that the narrativity of the text—the story, the representation—nearly disappears. The ostensible object, the narrative, is strung out, thin, and incidental to the substantial, monumental object: the two great enclosing parentheses that themselves with the text constitute the essential narrativity. The reading of this text must be a rewriting, or misreading, for Joyce has waived any rights to authority with respect to meaning and representation. Ambiguity is not only rampant; it is the rule.

The work is littered with traces of yet another Jack: non-bipolar logic, recurring themes, submerged allusion, absences of beginnings and endings, an intensification of the difference in the written and the spoken, and the continual play of polysemy and ambiguity. "And shall not Babel be with lebab? And he war" (*FW*, 258.11-12).

Because of the nature of the text, reading and writing approach identity. In encoding, Joyce was decoding; in constructing the text of *Finnegans Wake*, Joyce was deconstructing the text of Western culture; in decoding or deconstructing the text, the reader necessarily constructs codes herself or himself. These codes take the forms of apparatus, or machines, which contain within them the ghost of architecture.

"IN THE fields with which we are concerned, knowledge comes only in flashes. The text is the thunder rolling long afterward" (Benjamin, "N," N 1, 1).

> This construction is an expanded version of a paper presented at the International Association for Philosophy and Literature Conference, Lawrence, KS, May, 1987 and first published in *Assemblage: A Critical Journal of Architecture and Design Culture*, 5 (Feb. 1988). Reprinted with permission from MIT Press.

Notes

1. From the *Guidebook* to No. 13 Lincoln's Inn Fields, London.

2. James Joyce, *Finnegans Wake*, hereinafter designated *FW* in the text.

3. The river Liffey flows through the landscape of *Finnegans Wake* in many guises, most frequently that of Anna Livia Plurabelle (ALP), and is usually coded by "LIF" or "LIV" in the text.

4. Johann Wilhelm Ritter, cited by Walter Benjamin in *The Origin of German Tragic Drama*, p. 214.

5. This is a distillation of Benjamin's concept of allegory in *The Origin of German Tragic Drama*.

6. Fredric Jameson, "Third World Literature in the Era of Multinational Capitalism," pp. 65-88.

7. From a letter written by Soane, cited in Sir John Summerson et al., *John Soane*.

8. Summerson, "The Soane Museum," in *John Soane*, p. 36.

9. Franz Kafka, "In the Penal Colony," p. 202.

10. Here, I have "bilked the best." The Jacks are lifted from Guy Davenport, "The House That Jack Built," pp. 45-60.

11. Benjamin, "N [Theoretics of Knowledge; Theory of Progress]," N 7, 7.

12. Robert Segrest and Jennifer Bloomer, editorial statement from "Without Architecture," special issue of *Art Papers*, p. i.

13. Unauthorized quotation.

14. Davenport, "The House That Jack Built," n. 23.

15. See Paul Ricoeur, *Time and Narrative*, vol. l, trans. Kathleen McLaughlin and David Pellauer (Chicago: University of Chicago Press, 1984).

16. The resemblance of *Finnegans Wake* to architecture has been noted by Bernard Tschumi and, not insignificantly, by its author.

References

Benjamin, Walter. (1977). *The Origin of German Tragic Drama*. Trans. John Osborn. London: New Left Books.

_____. (1983-84). "N [Theoretics of Knowledge; Theory of Progress]," (from *Passagen Werk*). *The Philosophical Forum*, 15.1-2: N 7, 7.

Davenport, Guy. (1981). "The House That Jack Built." *The Geography of the Imagination*. San Francisco: North Point Press.

Jameson, Fredric. (1986). "Third World Literature in the Era of Multinational Capitalism." *Social Text*, 5 (Fall): 65-88.

Joyce, James. (1969). *Finnegans Wake*. New York: Viking Press.

Kafka, Franz. "In the Penal Colony." *The Penal Colony*. New York: Schocken Books.

Segrest, Robert and Jennifer Bloomer. (1984). "Without Architecture." *Art Papers*, 8.4.

Summerson, Sir John, et al. (1983). *John Soane*. London: St. Martin's Press.

(photo by Robert Merrill and Maria Hall)

National Archives of the United States, Pennsylvania and Constitution Avenues

The banner reads: "Washington, D.C. Behind the Monuments." Inscribed on the building itself is the master-code for reading architecture: "This building holds in trust the records of our national life and symbolizes our faith in the permanency of our national institutions" (*see* p. viii for the contrasting style of the Canadian Embassy.) The permanency of social structures (i.e., social positioning of classes, races, and genders) relies upon a logocentrism which in turn relies upon its constant reification and valorization in architectural simulations.

(photo by Laura Rohrer Little)

Index